SPIRITUALITY, CONTEMPLATION

TRANSFORMATION

Writings on

Centering Prayer

THOMAS KEATING, OCSO
AND OTHERS

Lantern Books • New York
A Division of Booklight Inc.

2008
LANTERN BOOKS
128 Second Place, Brooklyn, NY 11231

LIBRARY OF CONGRESS CATALOGING-IN-PUBLICATION DATA

Spirituality, contemplation, and transformation : writings
on centering prayer / Thomas Keating and others.
    p. cm.
Includes bibliographical references.
ISBN-13: 978-1-59056-110-2 (alk. paper)
ISBN-10: 1-59056-110-4 (alk. paper)
1. Contemplation. 2. Prayer—Christianity. I. Keating,
Thomas.
BV5091.C7S66 2007
242—dc22

                                              2007042859

Printed in the United States

TABLE OF CONTENTS

ACKNOWLEDGMENTS   *vii*

INTRODUCTION "I'M REALLY NOT
RELIGIOUS": *Spirituality in the
Twenty-First Century*
BY THOMAS R. WARD, JR.   *ix*

1.   A TRADITIONAL BLEND: *The Contemplative
Sources of Centering Prayer*
BY THOMAS KEATING, OCSO   *1*

2.   THREE CONTEMPLATIVE WAVES
BY DAVID FRENETTE   9

3.   THERE IS NOTHING BETWEEN GOD AND YOU:
*Awakening to the Wisdom of
Contemplative Silence*
BY JUSTIN LANGILLE   *57*

4.   BEATRICE BRUTEAU'S "PRAYER AND
IDENTITY": *An Introduction
with Text and Commentary*
BY CYNTHIA BOURGEAULT   *81*

5.   READING LIVING WATER:
*The Integral Place of Contemplative Prayer
in Christian Transformation*
BY DAVID G. R. KELLER   *127*

6.   BINDING HEAD AND HEART: *A Conversation
Concerning Theological Education:
The Contemplative Ministry Project*
BY DAVID G. R. KELLER   *161*

7. CENTERING PRAYER AND THE WORK
    OF CLERGY AND CONGREGATIONS:
    Prayer, Priests, and the Postmodern World
    BY PAUL DAVID LAWSON   187

8. SEEKING A DEEPER KNOWLEDGE OF GOD:
    Centering Prayer and the Life of a Parish
    BY TOM MACFIE   211

9. SPIRITUALITY, CONTEMPLATION, AND
    TRANSFORMATION: *An Opportunity
    for the Episcopal Church*
    BY THOMAS R. WARD, JR.   225

10. KEEP THE REST:
    Practicing Silence while Professing Poetry
    BY JENNIFER MICHAEL   251

11. CHANGING YOUR MIND: *Contemplative
    Prayer and Personal Transformation*
    BY BRIAN C. TAYLOR   263

12. CENTERING PRAYER RETREATS
    BY THOMAS R. WARD, JR.   297

    NOTES   311

    ABOUT THE CONTRIBUTORS   327

ACKNOWLEDGMENTS

This volume consists of essays that were first published in two separate issues of the *Sewanee Theological Review* (*STR*): "Spirituality, Contemplation, and Transformation," vol. 50:3 (Pentecost 2007), and "Contemplative Prayer," vol. 48:2 (Easter 2005). The latter won the Award of Excellence at the 2006 Episcopal Communicators Conference for "Best Series of Articles on Theological Reflection." For this book, the essays have been adapted and edited slightly for repetition and style.

Introduction

"I'M NOT REALLY RELIGIOUS":

Spirituality in the Twenty-First Century

Thomas R. Ward, Jr.

"SPIRITUALITY" IS IN the air. Consider the following quotation:

> "I'm really not religious, at least not in any institutional sense," students often say to me. Then they add, with varying degrees of urgency, "But I have a strong commitment to spirituality."[1]

Mark McIntosh begins his insightful *Mystical Theology* with these words, which are familiar to those of us who serve the institutional church. In an atypical but spectacular error of judgment, Paul Tillich suggested in 1963 that, while almost anything else in religious symbolism could be resuscitated, "spiritual" and "spirituality" were irrevocably dead and certainly not likely to be culturally present again.[2] Yet here we are, some four decades later, awash with books that have the word "spirituality" in their titles! The most evident thing that they have in common is the *difference* in the meaning that each attaches to this word. Parish search committee members looking for a new rector often say that they are seeking a spiritual leader. When asked what they mean by that, otherwise articulate people fall back on the cliché, "I'm not sure. It's like great art. I know it when I see it." Martin Marty laughed at himself in what he called a "turn of the millennium" issue of *Context*, writing that he and many other prognosticators missed this emphasis on spirituality as they looked ahead to the year 2000 in 1967. He indicated that something unusually significant occurred—"a gradual and subtle but—in the end—drastic shift in sentiment and sensibility." [3]

The revival of contemplative dimensions of the Christian gospel is a remarkable part of this larger phenomenon, and the centering prayer movement is a major manifestation of the contemplative revival. What distinguishes this movement from many of the current spiritualities is its grounding in the Christian tradition and the institutional church. It is as if some of our buried treasures are being discovered, brought to life, and put to use. One thinks of *The Cloud of Unknowing*, for instance, or of the *Spiritual Espousals* of Jan van Ruysbroeck. As important as our rediscovery of such texts is, even more important are specific practices that emerge from them and the tradition they embody. Centering prayer as taught by Thomas Keating is one such practice.

The centering prayer movement is a responsible attempt on the part of laity, parish clergy, monks, and seekers to respond to the obvious spiritual hunger of our day. This book offers a glimpse into this movement through the eyes of some faithful participants. From my perspective this movement offers one good way to maintain the institutional integrity of our tradition while we open ourselves to the Holy Spirit, that beauty ever ancient and ever new is the source of all spirituality.

✷

On October 12, 2005, Thomas Keating addressed my class of juniors at The School of Theology during a visit to the Sewanee Mountain. This was a one-semester class that had as its title "Spirituality for Ministry." We read several books together and had much conversation, but the central focus of the class was to encourage these prospective priests to develop a deep, regular life of personal prayer. When I told Keating what my overall intention was, I did not ask him to address any particular theme in this session. I wanted to leave him free to say what he would to the group. In the course of his presentation he made the following comments, among others:

> The Christian religion is primarily about a transformation of consciousness. This takes spiritual practice and the cultivation of wisdom. In another time this was called cultivating the supernatural organism, what Paul called "a new creation." So the main thing is to be transformed into God, what the early church called deification, *theosis*, divinization.

He went on to develop this theme in more detail.

Later in the refectory over lunch, Keating and Christopher Bryan talked about what became the Pentecost 2007 issue of the *Sewanee Theological Review* (see "Acknowledgments") and what the theme should be. Bryan said, "What about 'transformation?' That was the subject of the class. It is certainly timely and appropriate. I think it would provide a good theme for our next issue devoted to contemplation." And so the issue of *STR* began to take shape.

"Do not be conformed to this world, but be transformed by the renewing of your minds, so that you may discern what is the will of God—what is good and acceptable and perfect" (Rom. 12:2). We know we ought to be transformed. In the depths of our hearts we know that we have been transformed in our baptisms. But we also know that we are works in progress, that God has more transforming work to do in us.

Through our knowing Christ in the Paschal Mystery, God transforms us. And by God's grace through the liturgy—and in personal prayer beyond the liturgy—we make ourselves available for Christ Jesus to continue to make us his own.

If the main theme of this book is transformation, a secondary and related theme is contemplation. For Thomas Keating and many others, contemplation is a means to the transformation that Paul describes. As Keating said in that class on that day, the tradition tells us that we need a spiritual practice that will open us to the transforming power of God.

Chapter 1

A TRADITIONAL BLEND:
The Contemplative Sources of Centering Prayer

Thomas Keating, OCSO

S OME PEOPLE USE herb tea or a blend of herb teas. It seems to me that the Christian contemplative tradition can be compared to a blend of the finest herb teas. Thus *The Cloud of Unknowing* is one such tea. Others include the "Jesus Prayer" of the Eastern Orthodox tradition, *lectio divina* as practiced by the monastics of the early Middle Ages, aspirations (repetition of phrases from scripture or one's own devotion), being in God's presence in pure faith, and turning to God in love as recommended by Saint John of the Cross. Centering prayer is a blend of elements drawn from all these traditions. A primary source is *The Cloud of Unknowing*, but we have incorporated other "teas" to establish a special blend.

While developing a special blend of herb teas from the Christian tradition, centering prayer has also tried to place this teaching in dialogue with the psychological discoveries of our time (especially our awareness of what we call "the unconscious"), as well as with the insights of other contemporary sciences such as quantum mechanics and the "new physics." Centering prayer has learned from Eastern methods the importance of the body's posture and a proper method of breathing, without incorporating their particular belief systems or copying their precise practices—somewhat like adding a touch of sugar or milk to a cup of tea! The tea is still considered tea, even with a dash of milk or sugar, is it not?

The conceptual background of centering prayer restates in contemporary terms the apophatic tradition of the desert fathers and mothers, Pseudo-Dionysius, the Hesychasts of the Eastern Orthodox tradition, and blends significant elements from Saint John of the Cross, especially his teaching on the dark nights of sense and spirit and his lengthy advice for the passage from discursive meditation (devout reflections) to contemplation.[1]

In addition, centering prayer incorporates Saint Francis de Sales's spirit of gentleness; Jean-Pierre de Caussade's attitude of total self-abandonment to God; the clarity of the spiritual discernment of the Venerable Francis Paul Liebermann; the theology of humility and of the personal love of Christ of Saint Bernard of Clairvaux, William of Saint-Thierry, and other medieval Cistercians; the mysticism of Saint Gregory of Nyssa, Saint Gregory the Great, and the Rhineland mystics; the boundless confidence in God of Saint Thérèse of Lisieux, along with her extraordinary insight into the Gospel of Jesus Christ; the charm, humanity, humor, and wisdom of Saint Teresa of Ávila; the liberty of spirit of Saint Philip Neri; and the salty wisdom of the fourth-century desert fathers and mothers.

In short, centering prayer is a blending of the finest elements of the Christian contemplative tradition with an eye to reducing contemporary obstacles to contemplation, especially the tendency to over-activism, that is, to put too much confidence in our own efforts, or over-intellectualism, which is too much dependency on concepts in our efforts to approach God.

Some traditional methods of prayer are meant for beginners and are only for temporary use. An important aspect of the spiritual journey is that our choices expand beyond good and evil and become choices between good, better, and best. Someone might ask, "How can I be asked to give up something that is as precious to me as my special devotions?" The answer may be, "God wants to give you something better." Later you may be asked to give up all methods leading to contemplative prayer in order to receive what is better still: infused contemplation. The desire for God invites us to ever more mature ways of relating to God as our love for God increases. There is nothing wrong with our old ways of prayer; they are just inadequate for the ever-deepening relationship with God that is expanding in a way that corresponds to our growth in humility, self-knowledge, and divine love.

Following is a list of important aspects of the centering prayer practice and their sources in the tradition:

One. Practice: choosing a place of external solitude. Source: Jesus' exhortation to enter into our inner room, close the door, and pray to our Father in secret (Matt. 6:6).

I will quote the commentary on that text by Abba Isaac in Chapter Nine of John Cassian's *Conferences*, a fourth-century treatise about the spiritual practices of the desert fathers and mothers of Egypt, who peopled the deserts south of Alexandria (now Cairo) both as hermits and cenobites (monks and nuns living in communities).

> We need to be especially careful to follow the Gospel precept which instructs us to go into our [inner] room and shut the door so that we may pray to our Father. And this is how we can do it.

> We pray with the door shut whenever we withdraw our hearts completely from the tumult and noise of our thoughts and our worries

and when secretly and intimately we offer our prayers to the Lord.

We pray with the door shut when, without opening our mouths, and in perfect silence, we offer our petitions to the one who pays no attention to words but looks hard at our hearts.

We pray in secret when, in our hearts alone and in our recollected spirits, we address God and reveal our wishes only to him and in such a way that the hostile powers themselves have no inkling of their nature. Hence, we must pray in utter silence to insure that the thrust of our pleading be hidden from our enemies who are especially lying in wait to attack us during our prayer. In this way, we shall fulfill the command of the prophet Micah, "Keep your mouth shut from the one who sleeps on your breast." [2]

Two. Practice: gentleness toward unwanted thoughts, feelings, perceptions, and impressions of any kind during prayer. For example, Saint Francis de Sales in *Introduction to the Devout Life*: "Act with great patience and gentleness toward ourselves.... We must not be annoyed by distractions or our failures but start over without any further ado." [3]

Three. Practice: returning again and again to the chosen symbol of our consent to God's presence and action within. The symbol may be a word of one or two syllables, an inward turning to God or

Jesus *as if* gazing at someone we greatly love, or noticing our breathing.[4]

Four. Practice: confidence in God's infinite mercy and unconditional love for us, both in prayer and daily life.[5]

Five. Practice: self-surrender and abandonment to God's will.[6]

Six. Practice: the various kinds of thoughts that may occur during prayer.[7]

Seven. Practice: purification of the unconscious. The dark nights of Saint John of the Cross, especially his teaching on the secret ladder of contemplation. Centering prayer owes much to *The Living Flame of Love* in which Saint John of the Cross writes that as long as we have not reached our inmost center, there is still progress to be made.[8]

Eight. Practice: the laying aside of thoughts during centering prayer. "Thoughts" includes any perception at all, whether bodily, emotional, mental, or spiritual.[9]

Nine. Practice: disregarding every kind of thought during prayer, even the most devout, as the ravings of a madman.[10]

Ten. Practice: recognizing and accepting the ascending levels of union with God in contemplative prayer.[11]

Eleven. Practice: humanness and humor.[12]

Twelve. Practice: continuous growth in divine union and unity. [13]

Thirteen. Practice: faith in the divine indwelling of the Most Holy Trinity as the source of centering prayer. [14]

Fourteen. Practice: the movement of faith and love toward God as the inmost center of our being: awakening to the true self. [15]

Fifteen. Practice: its unwavering Christ-centered focus, especially participating in Christ's passion, death, descent into hell, and resurrection. [16]

Sixteen. Practice: the ecclesial dimension: bonding with everyone in the mystical Body of Christ and extending love to the whole human family and to all creation. [17]

This is only a sampling of major sources, but it may give you a sense that centering prayer is not just one thing. It is rather an effort to provide a blend of the best of the Christian contemplative tradition and at the same time to respond to the needs of our contemporary cultural scene with its particular obstacles and hang-ups to contemplation.

Our psyche is like a reservoir that we need to keep filling with water. If we miss a few days, it begins to run dry. We may then fall into emotional turmoil that we cannot handle because we have no spiritual resources left in the reservoir. Continuing to fill our minds and hearts with the peace of Christ throughout the day is important if we are to maintain the effects of centering prayer in daily life: interior peace, good relationships, and less upsetting emotions.

A certain number of Christian practices have been on the shelf for centuries. By studying the spiritual disciplines of the other world religions, we may be reminded of some that are present in our tradition but which we have not been using. Saint Justin Martyr is quoted as saying "Whatever is true belongs to me as a Christian." This is what the fathers of the church, Christian contemplatives, and certain theologians have believed and practiced down through the ages. They have taken the wisdom available in their times and tried to integrate it into the Christian experience. The problem is that they have not done it enough. They did it with the Greco-Roman culture and its offshoots in the Western world, but we have yet to accomplish the same task with Taoist, Hindu, Buddhist, Jewish, Muslim, Native American, and other major religious cultures.

Chapter 2

THREE CONTEMPLATIVE WAVES

David Frenette

SCANDALS AND POLARIZATION within Christian denominations. Monasteries empty of young people. Efforts to find spirituality within church structures. Struggles to nurture spirituality within church structures. Christian fundamentalism and scientism that equally reduce mystery to black and white. Secularism, pluralism, and materialism. A supermarket of New-Age and traditional choices for the spiritual consumer. As Christianity faces these internal and external challenges to its meaning and message in a new millennium, one might wonder: "Where is God in all of this?" Is God still working in the tradition to bring people to the radical transformation that Christian contemplative teachers throughout the centuries have said is the heart of Jesus' message? If so, then how is this happening?

In the early fourth century, as Christianity became the religion of the Roman Empire, many men and

women fled the new-found status and institutional-
ization of their religion into the wild and empty deserts of Egypt and Syria. The God who found them in
the desert formed many of them into contemplatives.
Some became what are now known as desert fathers
and mothers, and their teachings were practiced and
passed to others as a living tradition of Christian
contemplation.

During this time God did not die with the changing face of Christianity and social evolution. Rather,
God brought forth a new contemplative movement
that shifted the meaning of what it meant to give
oneself radically to God. Becoming a martyr and
dying at the hands of Roman persecution in witness
for Christ changed into becoming a "martyr of con-
science" and dying an internal death into the inner
resurrection of the contemplative life.

This desert contemplative movement was not
anyone's plan or program. It was something that
happened in people who were somehow feeling
called by God to "lose their life in order to find it"
(Matt. 10:39). Attaining the transformed life that
they sought in Christ, not a degree or ordination,
was the qualification for becoming an *Abba* (father)
or *Amma* (mother). Their wisdom, life, and practice
did not emerge all at once from one person. Instead,
it unfolded over the course of several generations as
an expression of God's action in the lives and teachings of significant individuals—such as Anthony of

the Desert—and in small communities—such as Pachomius's *koinonia*: communities of brethren.[1] In the midst of the social and religious changes of the fourth and fifth centuries, God acted in people's commitment to contemplative life and practice, bringing to the surface over time a living witness to the contemplative dimension of the Gospel. This witness later became the inspiration for the monastic contemplative life of Christianity in both western and eastern Europe. Is a similar renewal happening now in a very different world? I believe it is.

I believe that God is drawing forth a new movement suitable for today's Christian contemplative life and practice. This can provide a Christian spiritual foundation for the globalizing world, just as the desert contemplative life did for the newly Christianized Roman world and as monastic life did later for the medieval European world. The real impact of this contemplative movement, along with its details, will only be known from the long view of history. Yet its shape and contours already begin to be identifiable because it has been developing for at least two generations. The intention of this chapter is to identify some of its qualities so that others might recognize it, deepen their participation in it, and allow God to unfold it further in their own personal commitment to Christ through contemplative prayer.

Because I believe the essential quality of this movement is to practice contemplation in ordinary life, in this chapter I use the term "incarnational contemplation" to describe it. In a manner that may be realized by prayer and God's grace, the life of God is inseparable from ordinary human life. This is the witness of the whole of scripture and, in particular, of the Incarnation (John 1:1–18). I also use the metaphor of repeated waves breaking on the beach to describe the phenomenon of God's action in bringing to the surface this contemplative movement. This movement has emerged in human experience and has been expressed by human creativity and actions, but it has a divine source. It has particular relevance for contemporary seekers and that, I believe, is the reason for its appearing.

I shall try to describe what I see as the first two waves of this new movement by looking at the work of two recent Christian contemplatives who have lived it: Thomas Merton and Thomas Keating. Some selections from their writings will be cited to highlight three of its major themes: its contemplative practice, its psychological theory, and its social/communal context. Then, some examples of how these three themes are currently developing in a "third wave" will be offered, along with an invitation for us all to identify further such examples from our own experience.

In two thousand years of Christian tradition, contemplative renewal has always emerged as an original inspiration suited to a changed society. It is first articulated, then embodied in communal practice, and then developed across successive generations. Its founders' spiritual practice and life are thus tested and refined as their lived experience is passed to their successors. Thus, the Spirit of God is expressed in each generation, building on what has gone before. Wisdom is transmitted on the foundation of mature contemplative practice so that the renewal has in it something that is truly a part of God's action, working through people. Like waves that break upon a beach, each new wave is formed of the same water as previous waves, yet in a new way. And it is only after this has occurred across a few generations that a new expression of contemplative life can be said to be mature, and so become a "tradition" in itself. I believe that this is what God is doing now.

THOMAS MERTON AND THE FIRST WAVE

In the past fifty years, as internal and external challenges to Christianity have grown, so too has interest in contemplative spirituality. Beginning in the 1950s, books on Christian spirituality and contemplation became bestsellers. Many authors, teachers, and directors have written about spirituality. The Trappist monk Thomas Merton's books were particularly helpful in communicating to people outside the monastery the contemplative essence of that lifestyle. In retrospect, this period of time and this activity of describing and animating the contemplative life, can be seen as the beginning, the "first wave" of a renewal in contemplative Christianity.

In 1941, at the age of twenty-six, Thomas Merton entered a strict contemplative monastery. His spiritual life was formed by the traditional spirituality of one of the most austere and cloistered Christian monastic orders. He gave himself to it wholeheartedly and, through his writings, became an apologist and voice for monasticism. Yet, as he matured in his spirituality, he also became critical of monastic institutional rigidity. His interests as a writer and as a spiritual seeker expanded outside the monastery to explore Eastern religions, art, peace and social justice issues, experiments in monastic life, and a deepening personal call to more solitude. He died in 1968 in Bangkok while on an extended Asian pilgrimage to meet with Eastern spiritual teachers.

For the previous few centuries, the contemplative tradition in Christianity had existed primarily in monasteries. [2] Using his gifts as a writer, Merton described contemplative spirituality in ways that brought it to new life. Merton had a way of writing that was very personal and intimate, inviting the reader's identification with his own experiences, struggles, and life-journey. Some were inspired to become contemplative monks or nuns. Many others were (and continue to be) encouraged to recognize in the quiet of their own hearts the "seeds of contemplation" that God had planted in them.

This was the great benefit of Merton's books for me when I read them during my own conversion as a young man in the 1970s. I was not raised with any religious orientation. I began practicing Eastern meditation in college only to begin having inner experiences of Christ's silent and loving presence. Reading Merton brought to life for me the Christian contemplative tradition and the great spiritual masters of the past. Although Merton was by then no longer alive, he helped me to pursue contemplative prayer and begin my Christian journey. The fact that he was a convert himself, had a deep appreciation of the world's contemplative traditions, questioned religious and social structures, and was fully human in his search for God were all pathways for my conversion. I believe that Merton and other spiritual writers and teachers continue to be needed guides to the contemplative life for many today.

In speaking of contemplation, Merton writes:

> Contemplation is essentially a listening in silence, an expectancy. And yet in a certain sense, we must truly begin to hear God when we have ceased to listen. What is the explanation of this paradox? Perhaps only that there is a higher kind of listening, which is not an

> attentiveness to some special wavelength, a
> receptivity to a certain kind of message, but
> a general emptiness that waits to realize the
> fullness of the message of God within its own
> apparent void.... He waits on the Word of God
> in silence, and when he is "answered," it is not
> so much by a word that bursts into his silence.
> It is by his silence itself suddenly, inexplica-
> bly revealing itself to him as a word of great
> power, full of the voice of God. [3]

Since the contemplative experience is so innate, so natural to us, Merton's words rang true to many. He wrote extensively about monastic contempla- tive life. Yet because the contemplative experience by its very nature transcends the practices that facilitate it, his writings also brought to life the essence of contemplation beyond monastic prac- tice. Monastic practices—*lectio divina*, the liturgy of the hours, the Eucharist, the silence and separa- tion of the cloister—formed Merton's contempla- tive life. Yet, as he matured in his divine and human life, other things—nature, art, politics, human relations (especially with women), social justice concerns, and all the manifestations of human life—also became mirrors of God for him. As he grew, Merton experienced and began to articulate the message of what now can be seen as incarna- tional contemplation: that God and contemplative transformation are also in the world and human life, not separate from them.

A turning point in his life came with an experience in 1958, which became one of the most celebrated pieces of his personal journals:

> Yesterday, in Louisville, at the corner of Fourth and Walnut, suddenly realized that I loved all the people and that none of them were, or could be, totally alien to me. As if waking from a dream—the dream of my separateness, of my "special" vocation to be different.... I am still a member of the human race—and what more glorious destiny is there for man, since the Word was made flesh and became, too, a member of the Human Race![4]

From then on, Merton's attitude toward human life changed. He remained a monk. Indeed, he moved into greater solitude to realize his life's work, and yet he found himself more and more involved with the world, with human life, with people, and with his own humanity.

Thus, the first theme of incarnational contemplation is evident in Merton's life and mature writings: an emphasis on contemplative experience and practice that is oriented toward integrating the divine and the human. Merton also laid a foundation for the second theme: a theoretical language that unites psychology and theology as the container for this practice.

The cell, the desert, the mountain, and the cloister—these were some of the symbols Merton used to describe the place of contemplative encounter with Christ. He also began to use another term, the "center," as a more interior symbol, along with other ground-breaking psychological language. He wrote:

> To be "lost" is to be left to the arbitrariness and pretenses of the contingent ego, the smoke-self that must inevitably vanish. To be "saved" is to return to one's inviolate and eternal reality and to live in God.... If you succeed in emptying your mind of every thought and every desire, you may indeed withdraw into the center of yourself and concentrate everything within you upon the imaginary point where your life springs out of God.... Our discovery of God is, in a way, God's discovery of us.... We only know Him in so far as we are known by Him.... We become contemplatives when God discovers Himself in us. At that moment the point of our contact with Him opens out and we pass through the center of our own nothingness and enter into infinite reality, where we awaken as our true self.... From then on our life becomes a series of choices between the fiction of our false self, whom we feed with the illusions of passion and selfish appetite, and our loving consent to the purely gratuitous mercy of God.[5]

Merton began to shift from a theology of human sinfulness, a strict dualism of body against spirit, toward a contemplative psychology that affirmed God's indwelling within us as our truest identity.

Other Christian mystics have also expressed this. Merton, however, used the existential language of his time—that of selfhood—to describe the human condition, its psychological limitations without God, and the possibilities of contemplative transformation. Merton based this on the progress of psychology at the time. He and other theologians laid a foundation for bringing together psychology and theology around the contemplative life. A generation later others, such as Thomas Keating, would build upon this foundation a more comprehensive Christian contemplative psychology.

Merton's contributions were many. This chapter focuses on three essential themes of incarnational contemplation. Merton also significantly broke ground in setting the stage for the third essential theme of this movement: that of the social and communal contexts for contemplative practice.

Social justice, peace, artistic expression, interreligious dialogue, relating to the natural world, relationships, and community. For Merton, these were not separate from the contemplative life. Of course, a contemplative needed to discern appropriate ways to be involved in these activities. Action had to flow from prayer. There were many tensions about this in Merton's own life-journey as a contemplative who was very much a monk. Yet Merton's writings, especially those from the 1960s, speak more clearly than any other Christian contemplative writer in history

about how the contemplative lives in certain contexts—social, communal, and others, such as the
natural world. There is an essential need to express
the fruits of prayer in these contexts.

The monastery allowed Merton to be a contemplative. Yet his criticism of monastic rigidity and his
continued personal search to find ways to fulfill his
own monastic vocation helped open the way for later
experiments with non-monastic contemplative support structures and communities.

The purpose of monastic renewal and reform is
to find ways in which monks and sisters can remain
true to their vocation by deepening and developing
it in new ways, not merely sacrificing their lives to
bolster up antique structures, but channeling their
efforts into the creation of new forms of monastic
life, new areas of contemplative experience. [6]

Merton was acutely aware that external structures were meant to support inner transformation.
His personal struggle to live a more solitary life
opened the Trappists to reform of their strictly communal lifestyle. He was a contemplative at the fore-
front of his time, a time in which the old structures
were crumbling and new ones were yet to emerge.

Thomas Merton was not the only voice in the
first wave of incarnational contemplation, but he
was a clear one. He is representative of many writers of the last fifty years (and of many more who are
writing, teaching, and speaking now) who describe

the contemplative journey so that others can follow it. The more God is the source of a writer's activity, the more the author's talents and words are a transparent vehicle for divine life. This continues for many people to be the case with Merton. Perhaps it was God's unique presence in him as his true self, working through his talents and life experiences, that helped to awaken God in others. Once God worked through people such as Merton to bring the message and meaning of contemplation to the surface again, then there was a need for a system of practice and support so that those who did not live in monasteries could pursue the Christian contemplative journey. This became the second wave of incarnational contemplation.

THOMAS KEATING AND THE SECOND WAVE

Once one has opened to God in contemplation, one needs to practice contemplative prayer regularly, to receive support for living contemplatively in daily life, and to deepen one's understanding of life with God. Saying "yes" to the invitation of contemplation can deepen to saying "yes" to the contemplative journey. As God drew more and more people toward contemplation in the 1960s and 1970s, so it was the case that inspired initiatives for supporting the practice and path of incarnational contemplation emerged in the 1980s and 1990s.

Many excellent teachers of Christian-based contemplative practice in the last twenty-five years have contributed to the second wave of the incarnational contemplative movement. This shows that, rather than being the work of any one person, it is actually the work of God through many people. Thomas Keating stands out, however, for his work with centering prayer, a practice he actually co-founded with his fellow Trappists, Fathers Basil Pennington and William Meninger. As with Thomas Merton, Keating's work clearly embodies all the essential incarnational themes. Other notable contemplative practice teachers, who have also established extensive support networks for contemplative living in the world, include Fathers John Main and Laurence Freeman and the World Community of Christian Meditation, and the Reverend Tilden Edwards and Dr. Gerald May of the Shalem Institute. These groups have a strong presence in the United States. Over time, it will be interesting and important to see how other contemplative teachers and groups in other parts of the world express the unity and diversity of an incarnational charism—and also to see what happens as women become more socially accepted as contemplative teachers.

Thomas Keating entered a Trappist monastery in New England (a different one from that entered by Merton) in 1944. He became a priest, novice master, and served as abbot from 1961 to 1981, when he presided over monastic reforms initiated by the Second Vatican Council of the Roman Catholic Church. His position as abbot honed and expressed his gifts as an administrator and spiritual master. He retired from his abbacy after twenty years of service and moved to a smaller monastery in Snowmass, Colorado, that he had helped found in the 1950s. He lives there still. From there he began teaching centering prayer retreats himself, founded a network organization—Contemplative Outreach—to support centering prayer, and continues to present his teaching in spoken, written, audio, and video formats.

I first heard Thomas Keating in 1982 when he came to Berkeley, California, to give a spiritual talk. I remember leaving the event and saying to a friend that here, finally, was a Christian Abba. And I had not seen him in a monastery, but in Berkeley! I later wrote a letter to him, asking about some difficulties that I had been having in my contemplative life. I had become a Christian in 1981. Having practiced Eastern methods of meditation for a few years, I knew of the value of interior practice, so I began doing centering prayer after reading Basil Pennington's book on it. I was working part-time with children with developmental disabilities and was able to devote a good deal of the day to my spiritual practice. I was in my mid-twenties and looking at different monasteries because at that time a monastery was the only supportive environment of which I was aware for the life I was living. I was struggling spiritually because, aside from one spiritual friend, I had no support besides Christ.

Thomas Keating responded to my letter. We met shortly afterward. Because I was young, he encouraged me to take time in discerning a monastic vocation. He invited me on a new two-week intensive centering prayer retreat he was giving that summer, which I attended. Afterward, I went to his monastery in Colorado and, instead of becoming a monk, became part of the first contemplative community under his auspices, outside the monastery. For the next eleven years I lived and worked full-time in contemplative retreat centers and communities under his guidance. Like many, I benefited from the way that God has worked through Keating's own commitment to Christ through contemplative prayer, his life-journey and his human gifts.

CENTERING PRAYER
AS CONTEMPLATIVE PRACTICE

The main thrust of Keating's teaching is on the need and value of contemplative practice. He sees centering prayer as one way to reduce the obstacles to contemplative prayer. Contemplation is the essence of Jesus' teaching on the "prayer in secret" (Matt. 6:6).

Keating describes the contemplative practice of centering prayer as an "extract" of monastic spirituality. In the fourth century, Anthony of the Desert discovered and organized the four basic elements of the contemplative lifestyle: solitude, silence, simplicity, and a discipline for prayer and action. Monastic life is an environment designed to support the practice of these essential elements of spiritual health. Contemplative prayer combines these four elements in a capsule that can be taken twice a day. [7]

Centering prayer, like other contemplative practices, such as Christian Zen and Christian meditation, has as its focus an interior dimension. It is through this development of interior practice that the contemplative life can be fully lived in the world:

> Origen ... considered the Christian community in the world to be the proper place of *ascesis*. It was only through Anthony's example and Athanasius's report of it that the practice of leaving the world became the standard way to pursue the Christian path to divine union. Anthony had no intention of making this the only way to achieve it, but when mass movements occur, popularizations also take place, and these may fossilize or even caricature a movement. A new wave of spiritual renewal has to arise before the necessary distinctions can again be made. This may take a long time when movements have become institutionalized. The essence of monastic life is not its structures but its interior practice, and the

heart of interior practice is contemplative prayer. [8]

Centering prayer expresses the Christian contemplative tradition, especially as transmitted by Trappist charism. Thomas Merton used "center" as a symbol for the place of contemplative encounter with God. William Meninger formulated the method of centering prayer based on the fourteenth-century classic *The Cloud of Unknowing*. Basil Pennington used his gifts as a writer and speaker to present it to a wide audience. And Thomas Keating refined it as a contemplative practice and articulated how its practice facilitates transformation in Christ. He defines it as a way of practicing one's intention to consent to the presence and action of the ultimate mystery of God. His books—*Open Mind, Open Heart* in particular—describe how to do it. The workshops offered by Contemplative Outreach are a good way to learn it. The following are some extracts from Keating's writings that highlight the interior, psycho-spiritual dimension of an incarnational contemplative practice:

> Choose a word that represents our intention to consent to God's presence and action within us—it could be "God," "Abba," "Jesus," "peace," or some other word—and return to that word whenever we feel our intention growing fuzzy. [9]

All methods that lead to contemplation are more or less aimed at bypassing the thinking process. The reason is that our thinking process tends to reinforce our addictive process— our frenzy to "get something" from the outer world to fuel our compulsions or to mask our pain. If we can just rest on a regular basis for twenty to thirty minutes without thinking, we begin to see that we are not our thoughts. [10]

If you are suffering from a barrage of thoughts from the unconscious, you don't have to articulate the sacred word clearly in your imagination or keep repeating it in a frantic effort to stabilize your mind. You should think it as easily as you think any thought that comes to mind spontaneously. Do not resist any thought, do not hang on to any thought, do not react emotionally to any thought. [11]

The experience of interior peace is the sacred word at its deepest level.... So long as you experience the undifferentiated, general, loving presence of God beyond any thought, don't go back to the sacred word. [12]

The chief effect of centering prayer is to live from our center.... We interact better than before because we are not defending ourselves from people or circumstances, but living reality as it unfolds. Centering prayer, then, is not just a method of prayer, but initiates a process that involves the response of our whole being to the Gospel and its values. [13]

The Christian contemplative tradition has always included spiritual practices and interior methods. From the desert fathers and mothers, through John Cassian, to medieval mystical classics such as *The Cloud of Unknowing*, from the Hesychasts to the Carmelites, examples of interior prayer practice and method exist to support the exterior ascetical focus of the monastic contemplative life. Yet often the focus was on exterior ascetical practice.

Incarnational contemplation—in line with Jesus' prescription to "clean the inside of the cup" (Matt. 23:26)—first looks to interior practice. This roots its practitioners in the deeply contemplative disposition of receptivity. It gives them a way to relate to the thoughts, emotions, sensations, and other interior perceptions that usually exclude any awareness of the indwelling presence of God. Interior discipline then finds expression in exterior lifestyle and service, as one is faithful to Jesus' teachings. Service to others that is freer from one's own subtle self-focus, more rooted non-reflectively in God's love, is the fruit of contemplation.

Thus, centering prayer and other interior contemplative practices build on what Merton and others did in animating contemplation. They allow someone outside the monastery to take up the invitation that they received as a way of life. The second wave builds upon the first.

A CHRISTIAN CONTEMPLATIVE PSYCHOLOGY

Contemplative practice is always grounded in the context of a theory of the human condition and the spiritual journey. Monastic spirituality has its theory. Thomas Merton broke ground in articulating a new language of the interior life. Thomas Keating takes this further in formulating a comprehensive model of the human condition and Christian spiritual journeys: a contemplative psychology.

The concept of false self becomes more developed as the false self-system—the "consequences of original sin." Keating integrates an existential model, an evolutionary model, and a model of the Christian spiritual journey to explain why contemplative practice is necessary. Anthony of Egypt is offered as a "paradigm of the spiritual journey." [14] Thomas Keating's genius in this area is to articulate the traditional path of Christian contemplation in contemporary terms, in dialogue with modern science and the world's spiritual traditions. He draws both on modern theorists, especially the early work of philosopher Ken Wilber, [15] and on his own experience and insight.

Keating describes in poignant experiential terms the existential pain of the human condition without the experience of having found union with God. This is the result of life's inevitable wounding—in spite of the fundamental goodness of human nature.

The particular consequences of original sin include all the self-serving habits that have been woven into our personality from the time we were conceived; all the emotional damage that has come from our early environment and upbringing; all the harm that other people have done to us knowingly or unknowingly at an age when we could not defend ourselves; and the methods we acquired— many of them now unconscious—to ward off the pain of unbearable situations. This constellation of pre-rational reactions is the foundation of the false self. The false self develops in opposition to the true self. Its center of gravity is itself. [16]

The false-self system works on unconscious levels in adults to compensate for the emotional wounding of childhood. Because human needs for security, control, and esteem were not adequately met, no matter how "functional" the family system, these three needs surface as three "energy centers." They have their own hidden life and effects. They control the emotions, interior life, relationships, and even the most well-intentioned efforts to serve others.

The paradox of human life is that we are unconsciously "programmed" by unsatisfied early life experience to seek happiness in ways that are futile. The emotional programs of security, control, and esteem are very strong and subtle. Our conditioned "identity"—the false self—circulates around fulfilling these needs either tangibly or symbolically. Keating identifies the various ways and levels in which these needs can be expressed. For example, the need for security can be expressed materialistically in an overwhelming focus on possessions, emotionally in over-attachment to people, intellectually in the need always to be right, socially in the desire for status, religiously in a legalistic attitude, and even spiritually in an attachment to spiritual consolation. This is all to the detriment of true human freedom:

> The heart of the Christian *ascesis* is the struggle with our unconscious motivations. If we do not recognize and confront the hidden influences of the emotional programs for happiness, the false self will adjust to any new situation in a short time and nothing is really changed.... Whatever satisfaction comes from getting what the false self wants is always brief. [17]

Thomas Keating's teaching on spiritual practice is set in the light of his model of the human condition. Fundamentally, it is two-fold. First, because God and the true self also dwell within the person, beyond the activity and effects of the false self-system, a regular practice of consenting to this indwelling reality gradually roots a person in contemplation. Through the healing experience of God's presence in interior silence, true existential security, control, and esteem are found. The practice of centering prayer opens one to this experience. As a way of purely receptive consent to the Indwelling Spirit, it bypasses the false self-system and its mechanisms, and true happiness is found in God.

Second, because regular contemplative practice orients us toward the healing and transforming action of God, beyond any felt presence, the deeper roots of the false self-system are gradually exposed. The false self's motivation and activities are no longer being acted out and reinforced. Thus, one is purified and begins to live more from the true self—one's unique identity in union with Christ. Keating prescribes the discipline of a "letting-go" of the emotional programs and instinctual needs in daily life and in prayer to facilitate this. The letting-go in prayer is encapsulated in the simple practice of centering prayer.

The regular practice of contemplative prayer initiates a process of what Keating calls the "divine therapy." Here, Keating develops a new contemporary image for Christian transformation. God is the "Divine Therapist," the healer who directs the transforming process. Through the deep consent of sustained contemplative practice, God, like a good therapist, has the opportunity to heal the unconscious emotional pain of a lifetime. As the activity of the false self is released, God "breaks up" blocked wounds in the psyche, and psychological garbage is released from the unconscious into awareness. Centering prayer teaches one how to relate to this "unloading of the unconscious" via repeated consent to God in faith. Faith is deeper than the resurfacing emotions, physical discomforts, and thought-barrage that express the necessary healing dynamic.

Keating sees Christ, the Divine Physician, as healing not only personal wounds but also the deeper spiritual archetypes of the collective unconscious through the traditional stages (the "dark nights") of the contemplative journey. Jesus' own life, journey, and message reflect this:

> Shortly after Jesus was anointed by the Spirit in the River Jordan, he was led into the desert by the same Spirit to be tempted by the Devil. Lent is our battle with the same temptations. The biblical desert symbolizes the confrontation with the false self and interior purification. Jesus was tempted regarding each of the instinctual needs. He did not consent to them while yet experiencing them in their utmost intensity.... Having rejected the exaggerated demands of each of the emotional programs for happiness, he invites us to do the same, saying, "Repent." This is as if he were to say, "Change the direction in which you are looking for happiness. You'll never find it in your emotional programs for happiness. Let go of your childish motivation because it can't possibly work in adult life." [18]

Thomas Keating's presentation of the spiritual journey is comprehensive. He introduces his general vision and his dialogue with psychology with a question: How can we make "the rich Christian contemplative tradition available in our day with the kind of language, inspiration, and support system that will enable contemporary people to pursue the journey to the end?" He goes on to say:

> In developing this support system, I turned for a conceptual background to certain psychological paradigms because I think that very few seekers are going to start the spiritual journey today by reading the classics. I wonder if any would have started centering prayer if I had not put it into a psychological frame of reference that they could identify with. I don't think the study of the old classics is the way to start.... I tried to bring the Christian contemplative tradition into dialogue with contemporary science, especially developmental psychology, anthropology, and physics. [19]

Psychology—when it includes the spiritual depths of the human person—is the language of the interior life. It is also something of the "street language" of our culture. In this new contemplative movement, God has used it to help describe the fullness of the journey into union with Christ.

THE CONTEXTS: CONTEMPLATIVE SERVICE AND CONTEMPLATIVE OUTREACH

The third theme of incarnational contemplation that Merton helped to animate is the necessary contexts for contemplative practice in the new millennium. Keating also stresses the need for contemplatives to show the fruits of their prayer in the world and to develop new forms of community to support their contemplative life.

There are hidden effects of contemplative prayer for the world. It radiates a general transcendent peace to others. Offering specific intentions from union with Christ, in faith, also has a profound effect. Yet human suffering in contemporary society is profound. Through incarnational contemplation, the Spirit is also at work in the active restructuring of social systems that promote injustice, inequality, and human suffering. Divine life and human life are co-mingled. So contemplatives are also called to a more active response to human needs than simple prayer itself.

Contemporary problems are complex; the deepest human abilities and creativity need to be accessed to find adequate sustained solutions. This is the inspiration that drew Thomas Keating out of the cloister and that continually directs centering prayer practitioners forward as their journey and compassion deepen. Keating highlights hunger, war, the destruction of the environment, social inequality, and religious bias as some of the most pressing problems of our era. He writes:

> One cannot be a Christian without social concern. There is no reason why anyone should go hungry even for a day. Since the resources are there, why do millions continue to starve? The answer must be greed. It is, for most people, an unconscious greed stemming from a mindset that does not ask the right questions and a worldview that is out of date. Those who have reached the mental egoic consciousness perceive the necessity to be persons of dialogue, harmony, cooperation, forgiveness, and compassion. The problems of our time have to be dealt with creatively—from the inner freedom to rethink ethical principles in light of the globalization of world society now taking place. One of these problems is our relationship to the Earth of which we are stewards. At the very least, we have the obligation to pass on the environment intact to the next generation. [20]

Keating reaffirms that just as only God can heal human suffering, so only the contemplative dimension can truly change the world. Without its deep transformative effects in the person, new social systems established through social reform will be subject to the re-expressed energies of the false self–system. Hence, Christian contemplatives need to be responsive to the presence and action of the Spirit in the world as they continue their spiritual journeys. Keating calls service that arises from such contemplation "contemplative service."

Like Merton, Keating has been involved in inter-religious dialogue for over thirty-five years. In an era of terrorism and fundamentalism, he invites all to seek the unity that is the source of all religions:

> One wonders what the responsibility of the world religions is in this situation. Historically they have contributed to serious violence, war, prejudice, bigotry, and endless division. Yet more than any other institution, they have an obligation to address the problem of world peace and to emphasize the human values that they mutually share and proclaim.... If the world religions would speak to the human family regarding its common source and the potential of every human being to be trans-formed into the divine, a moral voice of great power would be introduced on behalf of the innocent and of the human family as a whole.[21]

Finally, one of Keating's greatest contributions has been the establishment of a communal support system for contemplative practitioners living in the world: Contemplative Outreach. Contemplative Outreach is a grass-roots service organization that provides written, audio, and video resources on centering prayer. It publishes a newsletter (currently sent to 50,000 people) that lists national and international centering prayer retreats, workshops, and events. It

ho _____ (www.contemplativeoutreach.org). It
m _____ who have been "com-
r _____ ers for introductory
_____ twork," it encourages
_____ ntering prayer and its
_____ roups. Such groups are
_____ denomination, and also
_____ ns.

Prayer class

These local groups function as autonomous units,
while maintaining contact with a board of trustees
and an international office. Contemplative Outreach
uses a "faculty" of experienced presenters to staff
advanced centering prayer retreats and to develop
new programs as needs emerge. While recognizing that individuals are formed by their respective
Christian denominations, it is an ecumenical organization and supports interreligious dialogue.

This organizational structure is well suited to
contemporary Western society's pluralistic, non-
hierarchical, and informational nature. It is similar
in some ways to other support-group service networks, such as Twelve-Step groups. It emphasizes
local, small group meetings that share and practice
a healing and transforming path, and thereby provide support, encouragement, and example to group
members.[22]

The effects of a transformational spiritual practice are in daily life. For incarnational contemplation, family, work, relationships, and community

are both the place of the Spirit's presence and the arena for the Spirit's transforming action. A communal support system needs to be oriented toward supporting contemplative practice in this world, just as it also needs to provide retreat and enrichment options away from it.

Thomas Keating uses the scriptural images of new wine and new wineskins to describe how God brings about contemplative renewal. What is to be done with the new wine of contemplation?

> If the new wine is to be preserved, new structures have to be found that are more appropriate than the old ones.... What will happen with the renewal of contemplative life among lay folks? We will see new forms of contemplative lifestyles that better serve the new wine with its tendency to expand. [23]

Thus, Thomas Keating's work represents a second wave of incarnational contemplation. It builds upon and extends the first wave and Merton's work. It was not that Keating based his work on Merton's: they never met. Nor was Merton the inspiration for Keating's work. Rather, I believe it more accurate to say that Merton's work, inspired by God, created an important climate of receptivity for Keating's work a generation later, also inspired by God. Of course, both were influenced by similar factors: Trappist contemplative life, the reforms of Vatican II in the Roman Catholic Church, and interreligious dialogue.

Without Merton (and others like him), Keating (and others like him) would have had to spend years educating people about contemplation before presenting a practice for living it in the world. This is another reason why I believe that the incarnational contemplative movement has a divine source. As another generation comes to life, it is important to trust in this divine source to continue inspiring people in a third wave.

CURRENTS BUILDING FOR A THIRD WAVE

These are three of the themes evident in only two of the people whose lives and work represent an incarnational contemplative renewal. Thomas Merton's books continue to dominate the "Christian spirituality" section in most bookstores. Thomas Keating continues to teach and write from his monastery. Contemplative Outreach is now entering into its own third decade of service. The work of these two generations of contemplatives continues to introduce people to practicing contemplation in the world.

I believe that there are already hints of a third wave of this renewal. It will probably require another twenty years before the shapes and contours of God's action in this third generation become clear. These hints, or currents, of the third wave have ebbed and flowed. Some are growing. Some have dissolved because the time for them was not ripe. I offer just a few examples of the third wave to close this chapter, and I invite you, the reader, to consider your own experience for examples.

THIRD-WAVE ANIMATION

The first current has to do with the sources of animation in the third wave. Because the Christian contemplative tradition was mainly preserved in monasteries during the last few centuries, it makes sense that God would work through monastics and monasteries to renew it in the first and second waves. As contemplative monks, Thomas Merton and Thomas Keating are living bridges, channels through which the Spirit has flowed from the cloister into the ordinary world. Now that the many people who practice contemplation in ordinary life are maturing along the journey, moving through the "dark nights" into deeper transformation in Christ, might there begin to be Abbas and Ammas who are also husbands and wives, fathers and mothers, clerks and attorneys? Even carpenters, fishermen, and tax collectors! And might there also begin to be more developed intentional communities, as contemplatively oriented as some monasteries are, in which Abbas and Ammas are formed and then guide others?

Whom do you know that you would consider an Amma or an Abba—that is, an animator of the contemplative life? What qualities do they show that make them this way? Using the imagery of this chapter, is the work that God does through them more indicative of the first wave (descriptive) or the second wave (practice and support)? Or are they beyond these waves, or beyond this imagery?

Mary Mrozowski is someone whom I consider to have been an Amma of the third wave of incarnational contemplation. She is the person whom Thomas Keating most credits with helping him with the inspiration and first founding years of Contemplative Outreach. Mrozowski was a businesswoman and divorced mother of two adopted children. She was in her fifties when God brought her to contemplation and the practice of centering prayer. Mrozowski and I lived and worked together for eight years at Chrysalis House, a residential community and centering prayer retreat center in New York State. I knew her as a woman of prayer and as a great friend. She was a spiritual mother to many in Contemplative Outreach. She was neither ordained nor formally educated. She never published anything. It was her life-story, her vibrancy and commitment to Christ, that qualified her in her charism. As someone once said upon meeting her, "I never thought I'd hear God speak with a Brooklyn accent." Although Mary Mrozowski died in 1993, she personifies for me what an Amma of the third wave might be like.

From Centering Prayer ...
Other Contemplative Practices

Thomas Keating says that the first task on the spiritual journey is to commit to the daily practice of contemplative prayer—through a practice such as centering prayer. This establishes a foundation for living the contemplative life. The task that follows is then to build on this foundation: "There are a number of practices that can help maintain your reservoir of interior silence throughout the day and thus extend its effects into ordinary activities." [24] Of particular importance are practices that work at dismantling the unconscious energy centers: "The reason that centering prayer is not as effective as it could be is that when you emerge from it into the ordinary routines of daily life, your emotional programs start going off again." [25]

Mary Mrozowski and Chrysalis House were both deeply grounded in centering prayer. The essential aspect of both Mrozowski's and Chrysalis House's charism was the development of other contemplative practices. Mary brought to life in her own prayer some of the practices that Thomas Keating suggests as complements to centering prayer. These came first out of her own relationship with Christ. They were refined in the light of the Spirit's action in the community, under Thomas Keating's guidance as Abba. After some years, as this Trinitarian container had purified them enough in the daily practice of the community, there occurred a discernment process about how they might meet the emerging needs of the retreatants. New programs were then designed.

For example, in 1988, Mrozowski and I felt that many of the retreatants who came to Chrysalis House were seeking something more spiritually formative, something more directed toward contemplation in daily life, than a centering prayer retreat alone. Over the next year we designed and piloted what became a nine-month course in "The Practice of Contemplative Living." A group of about sixteen centering prayer practitioners—along with the three, four, or five residents—would meet one weekend a month from September through May. Each month an essential aspect of contemplative living would be introduced by Mrozowski and myself, practiced over the weekend and throughout the month by everyone at home, and reviewed the next month. Thomas Keating came in December to review and deepen centering prayer.

We practiced the "Welcoming Prayer"—Mary Mrozowski's practice for embracing the Spirit's transforming action in all interior feelings and exterior events—inspired by the classic teachings of Jean-Pierre de Caussade and Thomas Keating's teachings on dismantling the false self. We practiced a form of *lectio divina* ("divine reading" of scripture), an intentional prayer for activity, a prayer of forgiveness, and also a simple way of contemplative discernment. Mrozowski's guidance in these practices was particularly inspired.

With this growing interior life, we looked at our lives, at the ways in which God was working in our relationships at home and in our attachments and addictions. By the end of the nine months, God had used the commitment to prayer that each person was practicing along with some life event—a change in job, a new relationship, an illness—to bring about a qualitative shift in being. We found God more in life, and we were better able to love others from this discovery. Mary Mrozowski was a skillful guide in this process, sharing her own experience and guiding others. The end of the nine months was celebrated with each person's symbolic commitment to her or his own newly formed contemplative lifestyle. The core community's commitment and prayer created a refuge for this to occur.

This course has subsequently been offered every year in the New York region, and it has been taught in the Denver and Florida regions by people who have practiced it for some time.

Having seen the effects of such practices and formational processes, supported by an Amma (Mary Mrozowski), an Abba (Thomas Keating), and a community (Chrysalis House), I believe that God is renewing other Christian contemplative practices to extend the effects of centering prayer into daily life. This is another current in the third wave. When I travel, facilitating retreats, and meet maturing centering prayer practitioners, those who have been faithful to its daily practice for more than a few years, I sense at the edge of their experiences the same kind of insights, inarticulate yearnings, and needs that Mrozowski and I heard in 1988. God is acting within them, within us, to surface a deeper form of contemplative practice, suited to the stages of the journey as they unfold in people, their unique temperaments, abilities, and life situations.

What forms of contemplative practice do you follow, or know of, that help you to live more contemplatively in the world? Have you taken part in retreats, workshops, courses, or deeper formational programs that are essential for your life with God? For Mary Mrozowski it was always the commitment to Christ in prayer, made concrete and practiced, that made the contemplative life possible. Similarly, it will continue to be the commitment to Christ, made concrete and practiced, that will make the next wave of incarnational contemplation possible.

Mary Mrozowski sometimes said, "Don't try to kill the false self; learn to dance with it." A possible trap of doing interior prayer practices, like a possible trap of doing exterior ascetical disciplines, is in thinking that our efforts are more important than grace. How helpful it is to have a psychological understanding of the difference!

Mary Mrozowski did not articulate a systematic third-wave contemplative psychology. She began to build wisdom sayings for life, which someday may become part of a systematic theory. Her statement encapsulates the essence of her attitude toward the human condition and its transformation in Christ as the spiritual journey unfolds. This is another current that suggests that in the third wave, as more contemplative practices and processes develop to help one live the contemplative life in the world, so too will a more developed contemplative psychological theory. From continued lived experience, deeper understanding can come. Reading this chapter you may have already had thoughts in this area. What psychological and/or theological insights would you stress or add to what has been mentioned?

I think that what made Mary Mrozowski's attitude possible was her focus on contemplative practice. Centering prayer is a practice for receptive intentional relationship with God—sitting quietly with eyes closed. Over the years, Thomas Keating has drawn forth the subtleties of its practice, which are particularly important for people as they progress through the stages and dark nights of the journey. The practices Mary Mrozowski inspired to bring the effects of centering prayer into daily life are ways of active, intentional relationship with God—accomplished after centering prayer in life. The "Welcoming Prayer," her primary practice for consenting to God in active life, was particularly helpful in realizing the attitude of which she spoke. In dancing with another, we are both receptive and active. Only by dancing with God can we begin to dance with the false self.

Merton himself spoke of this incarnational contemplative attitude in his own unique theological prose:

> If we believe in the Incarnation of the Son of God, there should be no one on Earth in whom we are not prepared to see, in mystery, the presence of Christ.... The Lord plays and diverts Himself in the garden of His creation, and if we could let go of our own obsession with what we think is the meaning of it all, we might be able to hear His call and follow Him in His mysterious, cosmic dance.... For the world and time are the dance of the Lord in emptiness. The silence of the spheres is the music of a wedding feast.... The fact remains that we are invited to forget ourselves on purpose, cast our awful solemnity to the winds and join in the general dance.[26]

LIVING THE CONTEXTS OF PRACTICE IN THE THIRD WAVE

As her spiritual journey unfolded, Mary Mrozowski grew more and more sensitive to social concerns. This was significantly expressed in her commitment to working with inmates at a maximum-security prison near Chrysalis House. As always, she broke barriers by gaining admittance to teach centering prayer there. It was a men's prison; the men formed a prayer-support group. Mary Mrozowski visited them regularly to share more about the contemplative life or to teach them another contemplative practice. She found her own life transformed by the encounter as Christ began to be present to her in the lives of these men. This was another way in which she witnessed another current in the third wave: continued living in the social and communal contexts of contemplation.

Although Mrozowski was an Amma to many on Long Island before she came to Chrysalis House, the community life at the house challenged, refined, and expressed her gifts even more. Chrysalis House was an experiment in contemplative community. A core group of from three to five women and men resided there full time, took care of the house and acreage, and staffed its retreats and programs. We committed ourselves to a form of the traditional monastic vows for a temporary time of contemplative training (one, three, or five years at a time) before returning to live in the world. Formally, Thomas Keating was the house's Abba. He visited for a few days every few months and helped us with our community life. Mary was an Amma and spiritual director for some of the residents and for many of the retreatants.

From 1985 to 1996 Chrysalis House was located at different large rented houses north of New York City. Part of its charism was not to own property. A simple daily schedule was followed by all: centering prayer three times a day as a group, additional time for personal prayer, morning and evening silence, work during the day, and a midday meal together with conversation. An "extended family" of retreatants from the area and beyond gradually formed, people who liked coming periodically to a functioning community that was living the same contemplative practice as they did. Many of its practices and programs were disseminated throughout the Contemplative Outreach network. Although it closed in 1996, Chrysalis House exemplified in some ways what a deeper form of community in the third wave might be like. To hold together over time, a spiritual network of small groups needs more developed communities of practice, just as strands of a spider's web need to be tied together at central points.

Why did Chrysalis House close? There are many levels at which this question could be answered. The community did continue for three years after Mary Mrozowski's death, growing and changing. I think that its essential charism was in being a place where the right people and the right conditions existed for God to reveal some helpful practices and processes in incarnational contemplation. It was a laboratory by Contemplative Outreach; quite a few people there were touched by the Spirit and furthered their own journeys. As they have grown in prayer some have begun sharing these contemplative practices with others.

In retrospect, though, I think that Chrysalis House's community life and spirituality had a cloistered flavor. We never emerged into a community fully integrated into the world. Thomas Keating once remarked that our contemplative practice and discipline was as intense as any monastery with which he was familiar. To do that, we relied on one rather strict semi-monastic lifestyle. After a valuable period of focused spiritual training, there was no other more integrated lifestyle possible at Chrysalis House for expressing the fruits of that training. So people were trained and left to live in ordinary life. Still, Chrysalis House was ahead of its time in the 1980s. It may have been a seedbed for other communities that are more fully expressive of the third wave.

Are you familiar with any contemplative communities like this? What people do you know who are drawing closer to a third-wave vision in their desire for contemplative community? Bernard McGinn writes that the community life of one of the greatest non-monastic contemplative renewals in Christian history, the Beguines of medieval Europe, developed in four stages and across successive generations. First there were women following contemplative prayer without a lot of connection with others of like mind. Second, some of the women formed church-based groups. Third, some of these groups formed small households to live together. Later, some formed larger communities that began to resemble religious houses.[27] Like waves across generations! In a similar way, hundreds of years later, might not God be working through people to bring forth more developed forms of communities to support incarnational contemplation?

CONCLUSION

Consider how ocean waves form. After one wave crests, breaks, and sends its water onto the shore, the ocean recedes for a moment back into itself. A new wave takes shape out of the same water as the previous one. This happens slowly. The form of the new wave is not easily seen for a while. Yet, when viewed from the beach, the formation of the earlier wave helps one to identify the new wave as it builds. In the waiting one learns that another wave will come.

In watching the ocean from land, one also gets a sense of its timeless and renewable action. One's own view opens to a greater perspective. The first wave looks and sounds tremendously beautiful and powerful. As one gradually immerses oneself in the perspective of the ocean itself, one still experiences awe with each incoming wave, but one learns better the deeper life and action of the ocean itself.

Then there is the possibility of leaving the safety of land to enter into the ocean. The waters come alive. One learns to swim. So it is with the living waters of the Spirit. To see God's action over time is to gain a larger perspective. To plunge into the divine life through the practice of contemplative prayer is to learn a new way of being.

Many people today are seeking meaning, freedom, and deeper life. Their search is set in a rapidly changing world that seems unable to provide "truth" anymore. God, however, is as alive now in the Christian tradition as God has ever been. Then, as now, contemplative prayer opens one to a relationship with the living Christ. God is the "truth that makes you free" (John 8:32). In the last two millennia God acted through people to provide means to support this relationship and life. In this new millennium, God continues to act. This chapter has sought to identify a new movement in Christian contemplation that responds to the same needs for meaning, freedom, life, and truth that have always motivated the contemplative journey.

The name given to it here is "incarnational contemplation." This is a term that describes some of its flavor: a spirituality that emphasizes interior practice for life in the world; a psychologically sensitive theory of the human condition and the spiritual journey; and a focus on supportive community, social concerns, and service. Its growth in the United States in two generations through the work of Thomas Merton and Thomas Keating represents the first two waves of its development. A few examples of ways that it may be entering a third wave have also been suggested. This is in the hope that some may feel invited or encouraged to pursue incarnational contemplation further. It is by practicing contemplation—Jesus' "Prayer in Secret"—that we are "renewed in the spirit of [our] minds and clothe [ourselves] with the new self, created according to the likeness of God" (Eph. 4:23–24). In this freedom, life, and truth, God lives through each of us, more and more, in the world.

This new movement will continue to evolve in ways and in waves that are, for the present, unknowable. What seems sure is that, as with the contemplative renewals of the past, God's transforming activity mingles with and inspires human activity to shape its evolution. The growth of a contemplative movement itself is incarnational: divine and human activity, intertwined inseparably. I see this firsthand in Thomas Keating's and Mary Mrozowski's work. I think Thomas Merton's work is similarly sourced.

So we who are in this next generation can feel heartened that God will use our fidelity to contemplative practice in ordinary life to bring forth contributions to this movement, small or large, hidden or public. Gratitude that comes from recognizing the gifts that we have been given by God and by our predecessors is crucial. In these ways we can cooperate with God's project of continuing to provide, through contemplation, an interiority to Christianity in a new and changing world.

Monastic life will always do this, based upon the interior life of the monastery. Its rich traditions are like embroidered spiritual tapestries hung on cloistered walls of silence. God is present in its solitude, silence, simplicity, and discipline.

With incarnational contemplation, God is also present and active in the stucco and ordinary wallpaper of the everyday world's life, just as it was in Jesus' own time: amidst the warmth of a supper at home with friends (Matt. 9:10), in the joy of a wedding celebration (John 2:1), wrapped up in the play of little children (Matt. 19:14), and in the tears and grief of death (John 19). Practicing an inner relationship with Christ allows this world to come alive. God is present in the ordinary routines of daily life and active through them in transforming us. Ordinary life is where we are called to manifest this transformation, in compassion and service to a suffering, and joyous, world.

Chapter 3

THERE IS NOTHING BETWEEN GOD AND YOU:
Awakening to the Wisdom of Contemplative Silence

Justin Langille

SOME OF MY earliest memories linger around the delightful echoes of silence. Loving family members were my primary role models for trusting the rhythms of silence, teaching me to cherish this "secret" language of the hidden, Holy One, and to them all I am eternally grateful. My mother and particularly my mother's mother, Kathleen, were my great mentors. Grandmother Kathleen's house seemed to be steeped in a captivating silence. I often reflect back on that simple home on 42nd Street in the Sutro Heights area of San Francisco. It was always such a safe haven, perhaps the only place that I could really call "home" for the first eighteen years of my life because we moved so frequently as a family. I have regularly reminisced about that enchanting residence and how it was bathed so often in the quiet, rolling fog that congealed off Seal Rock Point near the Golden Gate Bridge. Grandmother Kathleen's home, surrounded by gentle fog, later became an image associated with the metaphor of "clouds" in *The Cloud of Unknowing*, the anonymous author of which eloquently promoted the value of contemplative silence. [1]

Even more compelling than grandmother Kathleen's tranquil home was her luminous presence. She was a gracious, gentle, and compassionate woman who had faced a great deal in life, and she exuded a comfort and trust with silence that made it inviting. She became my primary mentor, and her balanced influence taught me to welcome silence as a place of refuge within. Grandmother Kathleen was no loner or recluse, but a well-rounded and cultured lady, a great conversationalist, and a woman of deep faith who put the joy of others before her own.

In time I was blessed with other bright exemplars whose lives were punctuated by regular intervals of silence, stillness, and reflection. I later realized how their influence, though subtle and unconscious, was formative for me. In fact, such inspirational example led to my interest in priestly ministry. What I did not grasp until some years after ordination was that my attraction to priesthood was really emblematic of a much deeper longing for intimacy with God—and an even deeper "vocation" than institutional priesthood. At one stage of graduate seminary training, a "life of silence" seemed so alluring that I was strongly drawn to considering the life of a Trappist monk. But monastic life was highly romanticized in those years and much more challenging than I had imagined. I later realized that, although I was not called to monastic life, I had always been drawn to extended intervals of silence in daily life.

Silence is a curious resource in a world that seems to be growing noisier by the day. Serving contemplative retreats around the country, I have become increasingly aware of how few places are sanctuaries of silence. The latest forms of transportation have electronic voices. Automated doors and elevators "speak" to us. Answering machines speak for us now, somewhere above the hubbub of radio and television. Our MP3 headphones silence the public but guarantee that private silence is not needed, whether in the bathtub, exercising, on a mountaintop, by the beach, in the desert, or even at our desks. We have become so adept at multitasking and busying ourselves that we have almost entirely squeezed silence out of our lives. Even while driving we make "good use of our time" on the cell phone. There are not many places where we can just *be* without the world's hubbub. White noise has become the auditory counterpart to the nonstop explosion of visual stimulation that fragments inner peace. A brilliant Nigerian author and poet, Ben Okri, wisely summed it up some years ago by saying, "When chaos is the god of an age, loud, clamorous music is the deity's chief instrument." [2]

Clearly, there is a place for noise and loud music, as there is for ordinariness in our daily lives. Like all the best things in life, silence is best appreciated in its absence. The greatest feature of noise is its cessation, especially when prolonged and agitating. If noise has become the hallmark hum of the world, silence may be the forgotten harmony of the eternal. Meister Eckhart, a thirteenth-century contemplative, proposed this piece of therapeutic wisdom: "There is nothing so much like God as silence." [3] John of the Cross echoed a similar cure for the world's obliqueness from his own mystical experience when he said that "silence is God's first language." [4]

I have learned that it is one thing to be attracted to silence, it is another to appreciate that it points to something beyond oneself; and for that reason the more profound significance of silence is not so easily understood or embraced.

Those in ministry and servant leadership might well relate to the human tendency to "learn" valuable lessons too early, to learn "things ahead of time." This has been true of "holy silence" for me. Entrusted with the spiritual care of others, we are frequently placed in roles where the unspoken expectation is to have a greater grasp of the Holy than the people we serve. The common result is to be forced to understand spiritual matters intellectually "before our time," before we have actually *experienced* their hidden lessons and impact upon our lives. Perhaps expediency is the chief perpetrator, but my sense is that people pick up on our spiritual paucity either intuitively or unconsciously. And while I face this challenging reminder over and over again, I keep gravitating back to expediency, ignoring my own and others' soul needs, and I am left having to "wait for my soul to catch up to my body."

I am convinced that we have to work passionately to grasp the hidden wisdom of "holy silence." Part of this soul work is ensuring that such silence is not reduced to something superficial, trite, or simplistic. I have discovered that the wisdom of contemplative silence holds my feet to the fire, relentlessly pointing to my transformation, to *my* need to change, instead of demanding that others change first.

In all the major world religious traditions, contemplation and meditation primarily point to the letting-go of the small self, the ego self, the false self. The principal focus of such spiritual practice is the diminishment of self-inflation and self-preoccupations, the surrender of the fixation with "what I want out of life" or "what I want from God." This may be one reason why not a few steer clear of silence in our contemporary culture.

I have found that far too much of the language of "Christian spirituality" pales to pious platitudes without the integration of the "contemplative dimension of the Gospel." Theology, liturgy, morality, and doctrine all have a necessary place in the journey of faith, but each is incomplete without contemplative silence. The repeated lessons of the spiritual journey teach that the gift of contemplation is essential and leads to a wholeness that integrates all other values in life.

Some of the clearest voices, from the scores of those who promoted the contemplative dimension of the Gospel throughout our Christian heritage, were ordinary women and men who lived extraordinary lives of faith in the deserts of the Middle East during the third and fourth centuries. So many of their insightful discoveries offer a plethora of practical wisdom, even to this day. Purified in the crucible of everyday life, many of these desert ascetics fashioned indispensable "tools" to expose the delusion of becoming "spiritual specialists" ahead of time. Like challenging Zen koans, they coined wisdom sayings to clarify the difference between "mechanical devotion" and spiritual maturity. Their penetrating maxims are proof of the depth of their own transformation.

Amma Syncletica, one of the clear feminine voices of the desert, declared:

> In the beginning, there is great struggle and a
> lot of work for those who wish to come near
> to God. But after that, there is indescribable

joy. It is just like lighting a fire: at first it's smoky and your eyes water, but later you obtain the desired result. Therefore, we ought to light the divine fire within us with tears and perseverance. [5]

In seminary formation, my yearning for spiritual progress was rather naive, self-centered, and in need of great purification. I received a rather impoverished paradigm of spirituality that failed to challenge my quirks. It proposed that spiritual maturity could be gained as the result of rote discipline and a slavish devotion to "saying prayers." It was as if spiritual development was the result of a "pious computation" that went something like this: add up what you have accomplished, multiply by what you have achieved, subtract what you have surrendered, divide by what you have avoided—do all this and count yourself a "spiritual adept." This odd formula was dreadfully mechanical, thoroughly disconnected from life, and quite useless in the end.

Fortunately, Grace intervened and provided me several exemplary mentors, wise elders who served as compassionate spiritual directors and helped clarify that spiritual growth is neither a matter of pious mathematics nor a self-centered adventure. Over the course of three decades in ministry, these wise elders repeatedly affirmed the "wisdom of the desert" with its clear focus on a Christ-centered *kenosis*. They made it increasingly clear that any desire for personal

transformation must include a commitment to serve
the transformation of the whole human family.

Like myself, many beginners to contemplative
prayer fall prey to the idea that "contemplation" is a
means of finding God by withdrawing from others.
And while I have discovered that eremitical withdrawal is not the main temptation for those who feel
called to a life of contemplative prayer, a common
danger is the unconscious motivation to gain a certain spiritual superiority over others who appear to
be less spiritually "enlightened."

I recall various times when I was tempted to seek
a certain "spiritual advantage" for myself in ministry. It is not always easy, nor pleasant, to detect how
the ego-self dresses itself up in "spiritual" disguises.
And when the desire to be more advanced or superior
is finally faced, patience and gentleness are essential
to our growth. It is also a reminder of the need to
meet regularly with wise elders and "soul friends"
to keep us humble and honest. So many of the "illusions of spiritual grandeur" are *part of* the necessary process of our purification and transformation!
Thankfully, contemplative prayer heals every one of
these common illusions.

Contemplation is certainly neither a superior spiritual position nor a withdrawal from others to find
God. Rather, it is a gift of Grace to purify every false
motivation and to draw us into a deepening intimacy
with God. Since the whole of creation is already one

in Christ, our dynamic interdependence mirrors the call to be aware of Christ's presence in each precious encounter. What I have discovered, sometimes painfully so, is that this dynamic unity confronts my desire to serve others on autopilot, avoiding my own willingness to die to self. When relationships or events expose self-inflation and failures, these are opportunities and reminders to be vigilant with the purification process and to welcome every prospect for transformation.

Thomas Keating is one of the pioneering leaders in the recovery of contemplative prayer in our time, and founder of Contemplative Outreach, Ltd. I have appreciated his wisdom and friendship over these years. One, among many, of the abundantly helpful insights he has uttered in his public conferences is that two powerful dynamics take place in contemplative prayer: "Divine Grace steadily affirms the truth of one's being, one's basic human goodness, while at the same time Divine Mercy gradually heals a lifetime of personal faults, wounds, and failings." [6]

The practice of contemplative prayer is actually one of the most efficacious yet "hidden" ways to serve humanity by learning to simply be still and be centered in God. "Be still and know that I am" (Ps. 46:10). The goal is to know God, *as God is*, by getting my false self out of the way. This hidden knowledge is the fruit of my fidelity to "God's first language."

The awakening contemplative gradually becomes aware of the presence and action of God in the presence and action of the other, sees the face of God in the face of the stranger, hears the voice of God in the voice of the "enemy," discerns the will of God in the longings of one's own soul.

As chaotic and confused as the human race appears to be right now, it remains our primary instrument of transformation. The fidelity to a practice of contemplative prayer helps me discover a deeper capacity to recognize "everyday God" in the stresses, tensions, and challenges of daily life and ministry. As I enter the silent recesses of the "inner room" (cf. Matt. 6:6), Grace secretly teaches me how to let go of the need to control people, places, and events. I emerge from this holy center gifted with fruits of the Spirit, with an expanding capacity to *be* a greater presence of compassion, graciousness, and peace. I also learn not to be discouraged by my mistakes and failures, because life mirrors endless chances for regeneration. Once the consent to being transformed is given, every human relationship and encounter becomes a graced opportunity to empty oneself and embrace "the abundant life" that Jesus promises (John 10:10).

In welcoming my role in the transformation of the human family, there are moments of personal responsibility that motivate me to rise to occasions of true courage despite the waves of negativity surging all around me. The Spirit takes the lead in purifying my false motivations to serve others, enabling me to be more deeply in touch with the true self, the Living Christ within.

What I have discovered in my fidelity to interior silence is that contemplative prayer is not so much my finding God, but more my allowing God to find *me*; allowing Wisdom to direct my heart, giving me the strength to avoid manipulating others and controlling life. The graces of contemplative prayer teach me how to prepare a dwelling place for Wisdom to rest within. In fact, one of the greatest fruits of this "prayer of the heart" or "prayer of silence," as contemplative prayer has been variously named throughout the centuries, is the longing to pray more regularly. Just the *desire* to return to one's relationship with God is an amazing grace and fruit of this prayer!

As Thomas Keating teaches, the fruits of centering prayer are not experienced so much within the period of prayer itself but in daily life. Ironically, you and I are usually the last ones to notice the benefits. It is usually others: spouses, family members, close friends, co-workers, and neighbors who see the changes and fruits in us first. They may even verbalize their observations in words like, "I don't know what's different about you, but you seem to have changed." It might be said in terms similar to these: "You seem ... a bit more patient, less judgmental, more forgiving, less stressful, more compassionate, less angry, more at peace."

Such fruits give us the capacity to recognize the goodness in the other, and also to become more aware that what I learn from others is what is learned about myself. With such awareness comes the growing ease with which to drop anxiety, judgment, and anger.

The whole point of contemplative prayer is to open us more deeply to intimacy with the Living Christ. Christianity asserts that Christ became human so that humanity could become divine. Christ remains the Way into the "abundant life." This is the essence of our Christian identity, one in which we are invited to welcome the transformation of our being.

To those who have little or no experience of contemplative prayer, how does one make sense out of *praying without words*? I confess that the encouragement to pray without words sounds a bit perplexing at first. The phrase, "praying without words," seems to suggest that something is missing or possibly that this fervent expression might be rather inconsistent, paradoxical, or even contradictory. Many of us learned to pray by *using* words at a tender age, especially if we received good parental modeling. In general, the impression is that if you are *truly* going to pray, then you have got to *do* something. What we usually "do" in our prayer with God is talk (often beg or barter), praise, adore, seek mercy or forgiveness, and thank (though not often enough, we might admit). For most, the term "prayer" implies *using words* that express a wide range of thought and emotion.

Unless someone has lived with a great deal of silence or solitude, the encouragement to *pray without words* might seem to be a difficult stretch or an intense shift in one's relationship with God, at least in the beginning. Admittedly, a daily commitment to "praying *without* words" is quite a bit different from what we ordinarily mean by "praying."

Jesus' own teaching on prayer was intensely profound because it was primarily a modeling of his relationship with God, whom he calls "Abba," Father. Jesus' prayer included words, but it also transcended them to experience a heart-to-heart, being-to-being communion with the Father. Jesus must have experienced plenty of times of tender intimacy, perhaps even ecstasy and bliss, in his "communion beyond conversation." But it seems that the most compelling dimension of Jesus' filial relationship was his *kenosis*, his total self-emptying into the love of the Father.

Jesus' death on the cross is a perfect demonstration of this *kenosis*, and its eternal fruit is the obliteration of humanity's conditioned experience of alienation, separation, and disconnection from God. The early Christian church named these barriers to deepening awareness of God "sin." Christians hold the conviction that Jesus "died for our sins." But Jesus' passion, death, and resurrection were a *preparation* for a much more penetrating reality. The Paschal Mystery truly *is* expiation from sin, but it is also something even more profound. Christ Jesus exploded open the doors of humanity's awareness *and capacity* to embrace the "abundant life," a life of deepening *union* with God. And although this extremely crucial insight of Christian faith seems to be persistently missed, it is waiting to be discovered in the contemplative dimension of the Gospel.

The core of Jesus' Paschal Mystery is what was at the center of his prayer: the total emptying of himself into the *unknown*. Again, Father Keating says it well in his conferences. In the Paschal Mystery "Jesus gave up love, *for love's sake*." The complete surrender of Jesus' deep and tender intimacy with the Father was an integral part of his whole journey into the heart of love. By sending his Holy Spirit, Jesus gives his relationship, his intimacy with the Father, to his followers, so that, one day, we too might share in the fullness of divine union.

I am convinced, as are many supportive companions in Contemplative Outreach that the contemplative dimension of the Gospel increasingly liberates us to embrace whole new dimensions of intimacy. Again, the complete scope of the journey of Christian faith is not just forgiveness of sin in order to live a good moral life. The full journey is an invitation to embrace the "abundant life" of Jesus, a life of *divine union*. Eventually, this calls for the willingness to give up *one's entire self ... in the service of love*. What follows the death of the false self for the Christian is the surrender of one's whole self, one's *integrated* and *unified* self or being. This is not a loss of our identity but an awakening to its *fullness*. Contemplative prayer leads us to the fruit of mature faith that is *complete* self-donation, one that mirrors Jesus' entire journey of return to the Father. Perhaps only a rare few souls reach such completion in this life, but it seems essential that we become aware of the *complete* scope of the journey of faith.

Like Jesus, we have no certainty of *how* such self-donation will unfold. But our self-emptying is a share in Jesus' own *kenosis* and gives us his "assurance" of *where* it will lead, which is into eternal, loving union with our triune God.

Jesus' *kenosis* put an end to the alienation that made humanity's longing for divine intimacy seem impossible. But what is worth pondering is that the goal of the journey is even more profound than "relationship with God." This is what the ancient desert elders, Christian mystics, and contemplatives of all ages have been trying to communicate as a fruit of their own experience. A relationship with God is an amazingly precious and essential place to begin. But the term "relationship" suggests that there still remains *some separation* between another and myself, between God and myself. In a deeply tender human bond, we expect more than friendship, and we hunger for an intimacy where nothing separates us.

The goal of relationship with God is *full union*, and missing that point is a colossal oversight. Perhaps the reason this crucial truth is so consistently missed is because it appears so much easier to remain in control than to surrender to God's love. We need to be aware of how practiced we have become at longing for intimacy with God while keeping God at a safe distance! It is like trying to drive with one foot on the gas and the other on the brake.

As our unconscious reservations are healed through contemplative prayer, we come to know that complete self-donation leads to a union with God that ultimately *transcends* relationship. Such union is so intimate that nothing remains "in between." Meister Eckhart experienced this profound truth and wisely declared, "Between you and God there is no between." [7]

Perhaps you have heard the following story. Once upon a time there was a salt doll who heard that the secret to lasting happiness was to travel the world and enjoy its many treasures. Soon thereafter, she set off on a journey with great excitement and anticipation.

One day, after traveling for some time, she came to the banks of a wondrous beach and found herself at the edge of a vast body of water. "What are you?!" she exclaimed. The sea responded, "Touch me and you will find out." Hesitantly, the salt doll stuck her little toe in the water. Immediately she experienced a wonderful sensation, but when she withdrew her foot, her little toe had disappeared. "What have you done to me?" she cried out. "Ah, you have given something of yourself in order to understand who I am," the sea responded.

The salt doll reflected on what she should do next and decided that if she really wanted to understand the sea, she would have to give even more of herself. She next placed her entire foot in the water, and everything below her ankle disappeared. Surprisingly, unbelievably, she experienced a wonderful sensation. Fearlessly, she continued walking further and further into the sea, losing more and more of herself, all the while coming to understand the sea more deeply. As a wave broke over the last little bit of her, the salt doll was heard to exclaim, "Now I know what the sea is! *It is I.*"

The longing for wholeness and union with God is a "holy longing" that we are invited to trust completely. It seems the reason we avoid this soul-hunger far too long in our lives is because unconsciously we know where it is going to lead: to our dissolution. With a sly twist of humor during his contemplative

retreats, fellow Trappist monks have recounted that
Thomas Merton would repeat this bold saying to
retreatants, "One thing certain about heaven: there
won't be much of *you* there!"

In the end, there remains nothing between the
individual soul and God. Again, "between God and
you there is no between." A deep appreciation of this
truth is one of the most compelling reasons not to
put words between God and oneself in deep prayer.

Those committed to a contemplative practice
know that the experience of "praying without words"
awakens them to an intimacy so complete that images,
thoughts, emotions, and words just get in the way. In
fact, words and images become barriers to deeper,
"pure prayer," prayer that is free of any self-preoccu-
pation. Anthony of Egypt, revered as the greatest of
all desert Abbas, once declared that "perfect prayer
is not to know that you are praying." [8]

As one enters into deepening trust and intimacy
with Christ, there is less and less need for self-con-
cern or self-reflection. Contemplation is a gift freely
given, as one ceases putting "anything" between
God and oneself. This is one of the traditional ways
that Christian ascetical and mystical theology begins
to speak about "mystical marriage." Certainly, we
need to be patient with our growth in Christ. The
wisdom of the ancient desert reminds us to remain
faithful in our relationship with the Living Christ
without seeking union prematurely.

Paradoxically, we often miss the essence of prayer: to pray is to "*be* in love." Life begins to change from that center when divine love is deeply welcomed. Most of our lives we seem to have it backward. We want to feel loved first and then we will get around to surrendering. My own haphazard attempts at love have taught me that it is only *after* I have learned to surrender that I even begin to have the *capacity* to experience love from the other. Like the salt doll, it is easy to forget who we really are because our attention is on the "treasures" of the world.

I have allowed plenty of "treasures" to get in the way of my relationship with God over the years. But one of the richest gifts of contemplation is the experience of divine mercy, "that it's all okay." Franciscan Richard Rohr says that this seems to be the "pattern of patterns" and "theme of themes" in the Bible. In the divine economy, God uses everything and anything—my failings, wounds, as well as successes and talents—to bring me to the experience of wholeness. It seems that God will go to any length to draw us into union, even to "break" God's own rules! Whatever the weakness, contemplative prayer gradually heals all obstacles to communion. This is why centering prayer has been such a rich gift and doorway into contemplation in my life.

Through the practice of centering prayer, we learn more and more that, since faith matures by progressive surrender, there is no reason to allow *anything* to come between God and ourselves. "Praying without words" is not something I do for God; it is rather doing *nothing* in the service of *love*. It is a kenosis that totally welcomes being transformed by love, into love. Such "mystical" language attempts to transcend dualistic language by suggesting that pure prayer is a "way of being." Evoking traditional New Testament language, it is a way of "resting," "dwelling," "abiding," "making one's home," and "remaining" in Christ.

To "pray without words" is to put the proper emphasis on *being* rather than *doing*, on *who* I am rather than *what* I *do*. In this expanding awareness, one finds *spiritual rest* in an unspeakable, unthinkable communion. Gregory the Great in the sixth century was one of the first church elders to refer to contemplative prayer as "resting in God." [9] In this resting, one *experiences* God in an intimacy where words become superfluous.

As one is drawn into communion with God, there is less and less of a temptation to "become God" for oneself. The Living Christ transforms our minds and hearts so that we embrace union with God not in terms of *identification with* God but as *participation in* God. The fruit of fidelity and perseverance in this "unspeakable communion" is the capacity to "see" God in every untamed and precious moment. Augustine of Hippo, who came to contemplation rather late in his life, once remarked: "The whole purpose of this life is to restore to health the eye of the heart by which God may be seen." [10]

With such spiritual vision comes the growing freedom that releases any need for mental certitude about controlling my life. As one rests in the "inner room" of centering prayer, there is a growing conviction that *"you know that you know that you know."* You *experience* the "Great I Am" that dwells in the very center of your being. In the Christian contemplative heritage, this is the "knowledge of the heart," where "heart" signifies the totality or wholeness of one's being. It is the integration of all human potentialities: body, mind, soul, and spirit, centered in Christ.

Contemplative prayer is all about embracing life, just as it is. Many of us fear that our lives are "not spiritual enough" because of the many regrets and worries that we have dragged along these years. However, centering prayer teaches us how to embrace the presence and action of God *amid* the regrets, worries, chaos, and messiness—and equally with the joys, achievements, and triumphs. To be "contemplative" is to be keenly aware that the heart of everyday life, with all its joys and pleasures, as well as its problems and chaos, is the principal domain of our spiritual practice.

Without practical "spiritual tools" to support us, we fall prey to all kinds of illusions and eccentricities. One of my common quirks has been to speed up the pace of my day, thinking that I will accomplish more, when in truth, my energy is merely wasted at a quicker rate. My soul keeps reminding me that my life-energy will be depleted if I forget contemplation in my everyday actions.

The usual current of the human condition is to go about our professions, ministry, relationships, shopping, and even leisure as if there were no natural contemplative dimension to any of these. And yet, no one benefits more from contemplation than the busy minister, the ambitious professional, the overwhelmed seminarian, the anxious father, the hurried mother, the distracted student, the ailing grandparent, and the restless neighbor. Silence, stillness, interior solitude, and humble service are all essential to life in Christ, and life is incomplete without them.

If you are discerning how to integrate centering prayer into your already busy life, please know that you join in solidarity with contemplative souls from all times and places who have discovered a trusted home in the silence despite the most chaotic of times and situations. If you are not familiar with centering prayer, consider reading *Open Mind, Open Heart* by Thomas Keating, [11] or contact the International Resource Center of Contemplative Outreach to learn where the closest contact person or prayer group might be. [12]

The ancient wisdom of the desert reminds us that, without contemplation, life is not complete and does not flow toward wholeness. The gift of contemplation integrates all other spiritual values. Our growth in contemplative consciousness, the "deep knowledge of God," as Saint Paul refers to it (Rom. 11:33), enables us to mature and to enjoy the "abundant life" of the Living Christ. The "secret," daily resting within the "inner room" gradually unveils what we have always already known: that "we are created for union with God."

A paraphrase of Jesus' proclamation in Matthew 10:39 might read: "The person who seeks only himself/herself will bring himself/herself to ruin, but the person who brings herself/himself to *nothing*, for my sake, will discover who she/he really is."

Allow me to relate a final story that conveys the freedom of embracing this "holy nothingness." Once upon a time, a royal banquet was being given in honor of a king who was returning home after an extended time away. All the guests had assembled in the palace hall and were seated according to rank. Only one chair remained vacant, awaiting the arrival of the king.

Out of nowhere, a disheveled old monk walked in and sat in the chair reserved for the king. The chief minister was instantly outraged; he angrily approached the aged ascetic and said, "How dare you sit in that chair? Are you an important minister, superior to me?" The monk responded, "No, I am more than that." "What!" said the chief minister.

"Are you the king?" "No," said the old ascetic, "I am more than that." "Then are you a prophet?" the chief minister questioned. "No," said the elderly monk, "I am more than that." "Are you God?," asked the chief minister. "No," said the monk, "I am more than that." Incredulous, the chief minister gasped, "What! How can you say that? More than God there is *nothing*!" "Yes," said the old monk, "and I am that nothing ... that nothing which is *everything*."

Contemplative prayer is the faithful and loving consent to "dissolve" into God's unconditionally loving being. Grace welcomes and then waits for our response. Even the "holy longing" that we discover in the depths of our soul is God's initiative. As Paul clarifies: "Likewise the Spirit helps us in our weakness; for we do not know how to pray as we ought, but that very Spirit intercedes with *sighs too deep for words*" (Rom. 8:26, my emphasis).

Finally, in the contemplative silence of "pure prayer," one discovers that there is nothing between God and oneself, and that to embrace this "nothingness" is everything.

Chapter 4

BEATRICE BRUTEAU'S "PRAYER AND IDENTITY":
An Introduction with Text and Commentary

Cynthia Bourgeault

MENTION THE NAME Beatrice Bruteau, and I dare say that most Christian contemplatives will never have heard of her. She does not have the "superstar" status of Thomas Merton, Thomas Keating, Bede Griffiths, or David Steindl-Rast. By her own choice she has preferred to remain slightly below the radar screen, but for more than forty years she has been one of the most powerful shaping influences on contemporary mystical theology, interspirituality, and contemplative practice. She has been a friend, colleague, and sometime mentor to all of those people mentioned above (and dozens more of comparable stature), and a teacher to thousands of appreciative students, myself included. Those who have had the privilege of working with her directly speak of the clarity and precision of her mind, the luminosity of her vision, and down-to-earth practicality of her contemplative practice.

Rigorously trained, she holds two degrees in mathematics and a doctorate in philosophy from Fordham University (one of the first women to graduate from this program). In addition to her highly articulate Christianity, she is also a longtime student of Vedanta and one of the early pioneers of East–West dialogue. She has written books on Aurobindo and Teilhard de Chardin, and she brings her deep understanding of non-dual states of consciousness to the mysticism of the West (as you will see in her essay). She and her husband James Somerville founded Schola Contemplationis, a center for the study and practice of the contemplative life according to the classical traditions of both East and West, with its "mind-bending" monthly newsletter *The Roll*. Her most well-known books are *Radical Optimism*, *God's Ecstasy*, and *The Easter Mysteries*.[1] She remains active as a teacher and theologian, and her vision just keeps on growing.

The following essay, "Prayer and Identity," appeared originally in *The Contemplative Review* in the fall of 1983.[2] It was one of the formative works in my own contemplative journey, and I continue to be impressed with its ability to cut through the rhetoric and sentimentality surrounding so much of the teaching on Christian prayer and to articulate a new vantage point with clarity and elegance. (Since the essay is now very difficult to obtain, I am grateful to Tom Ward, *Sewanee Theological Review*, and Lantern Books for their willingness to make it once again readily available.)

Admittedly, this essay may be a stretch for those accustomed to the primarily personal and therapeutic metaphors in which the contemplative journey has most recently been presented. Contemplative prayer does, indeed, provide relief from the false self and healing of the "emotional wounds of a lifetime." But even more powerfully, as modern neuroscience has increasingly confirmed, it begins to restructure the brain, changing not *what* one thinks but *how* one thinks. This restructuring, in turn, paves the way for the emergence of a Christianity at the level of "Christ consciousness": non-dual, non-judgmental, compassionately seeing the mutual indwelling (or "coinherence") of all things in the mystery of divine love. "Prayer and Identity" is a pioneering effort in charting the stepping stones along this pathway of radical transformation. Because some of the concepts and language may be initially unfamiliar, a brief commentary highlighting some of the major teachings in each of the five sections, as well as their points of connection with centering prayer, follows at the end of her essay.

❈

PRAYER AND IDENTITY
BY BEATRICE BRUTEAU

I

The way into the spiritual life is a matter of radical transformation. The further we progress along it, the more radical we realize the transformation has to be. The whole work of prayer is to cause, to control, and to appreciate certain transformations. Fundamental to these, so far as I see at present, is the sense of identity. The work of prayer is to transform our sense of identity. The Letter of James in the New Testament contains the following passage:

> If anyone is a hearer of the word and not a doer, he is like a man who observes his natural face in a mirror; for he observes himself and goes away and at once forgets what he was like. But he who looks into the perfect law, the law of liberty, and perseveres, being not a hearer that forgets but a doer that acts, he shall be blessed in his doing. (1:23–25, RSV)

We can apply these words to our work in prayer. When developed, the prayer state should first be a mirror and then a real environment of our natural face. It is a matter of looking with perseverance—

what I will later call *creative freedom*—into the perfect law of liberty until there is no more question of our looking away and forgetting our true identity. Insofar as we are not prayerful, we are at present in a state of forgetfulness; we do not know who we are.

Plato spoke of this mythically when he suggested that people choose the lives they will live before they are born and then drink the waters of Lethe, the River of Forgetfulness. After being born, he says, they no longer recall the larger context in which their earthly and temporal lives are set, the context that would have revealed to them a deeper dimension of their selfhood. Plunged in Lethe, in forgetfulness, they simply identify themselves with the particular roles which they are playing in life, as artisans or parents, merchants or politicians, poets or philosophers. If they are awakened by careful reasoning that presses on to intellectual insight, or by the quest of love for absolute beauty, they may remember that greater, transtemporal realm. This remembrance, says Plato, brings them to truth, to reality, called *aletheia*, non-forgetfulness.

The Hindus tell us that we are subject to *avidya*, not-seeing, and that we mistake our selfhood, confusing it with our ego-personality and our temporal history. They recommend the practice of yoga to bring us to realization of the Absolute Self. A popular Zen Buddhist subject for meditation is the demand, "Show me your original face, the face you had before your parents were born." The Taoists speak of our "original nature," which they liken to an "uncarved block," and they urge that wisdom consists in finding this again as our true identity.[3]

The problem of identity in all these traditions is clearly a fundamental spiritual problem. Prayer, therefore, the spiritual exercise, is in an important respect a matter of clarifying our sense of identity. And this clarification can be experienced as analogous to awakening, remembering, or seeing correctly.

Our difficulty is that we tend to think that we do see already, that we do know, that we are awake. It is just because we say "we see" that we remain caught in the difficulty (cf. John 9:41). This is why I said that the further we progress, the more radical the transformation becomes. At each level or stage we are still assuming certain things, still taking certain things for granted, without knowing that we are assuming them or taking them for granted. We so definitely see them as reality that it does not occur to us to question them, and it does not even occur to us to notice that we do not question them.

It is from the surrounding darkness of the unnoticed taken-for-granted things that certain notions will spring into light as each successive spiritual illumination takes place. Each time, we discover to our amazement that something we had all along supposed to be so is not really that way. Usually this happens in such a way that the entire ground on which the previous conception had been based is cut away, so that, while the previous affirmation is dissolved, its corresponding negation is made inapplicable also. One finds that the whole situation has to be reconceived from a new perspective or on a new foundation.

I sometimes think that the strange, mysterious, miraculous, and paradoxical events and sayings that the spiritual traditions set before us for our contemplation have as one of their functions to make us realize that we did not know something we thought we knew. For instance, in the case of the Eucharist, when a man can take up a bit of bread and say of it, "This is my body," one of the things that should become clear to us is that we have never known what any "body" was. It should force us to go back and rethink "body" in *all* its contexts, all over again. As long as we assume we know what "body" means and focus our attention on questions built on this assumption, we risk remaining embroiled in naive and even bizarre problems. When the "body" assumption is traced and transcended, these problems disappear.

Another example is the question whether one is free. This debate often takes the form of asking us to decide between being free to choose or else being necessitated or compelled to act as we do. Here the assumption is that the only kind of freedom there is is freedom of choice, that freedom consists precisely in the act of choosing. But if we can show another meaning for "freedom," one which is still deeper and even more "free" than choice-freedom, then the debate will have to be reassessed. In this case I have proposed the concept of "creative freedom," in which the origin and stimulation of the action is entirely in the agent, as against "choice-freedom," in which the stimulus of the act is in the agent's environment, which presents the alternatives and evokes the motive for choosing between them. One who exercises creative freedom may not experience choosing and yet not be compelled, and this realization should mean a more profound appreciation of what freedom, action, and the person as agent really are. This has something to do with the identity that I think we discover in prayer, and I will come back to this point.

Quite apart from whether one wishes to take up the particular *content* of these examples, this methodological structure is the kind of breakthrough that I am talking about as a movement from one stage of spiritual life to another. The point is that the question shifts its ground—usually to one more general and extensive—and when the ground shifts, the original questions either disappear or take a different form.

Applying this pattern of illumination now to the question of identity, I want to say that we *think* we know who "we" are, and on the basis of this secure knowledge, we debate whether we are weak or strong, good or evil, capable of changing ourselves or not, and many similar topics. Again, my suggestion is that, in the course of a developing prayer life, we realize that we have been making certain assumptions about our identity that are not true, not deep enough, not dynamic enough, or otherwise too limited.

II

What is our identity when we begin our series of transformations? We locate our selfhood in the experiencer of pleasure and pain. This means in the first instance in our human body of flesh, and then in the emotional nature of our human personality. We believe that "we" are the one who is comfortable or uncomfortable, who is happy or unhappy. This seems obvious and undeniable.

What happens then in prayer? The first prayer tries to correct and control the experience-environment of this self. It petitions the God who operates the environment to send the self pleasant experiences and to withdraw the painful ones. Sometimes it seems that these prayers are "answered," or granted, because a preponderance of pleasant experiences then follows, and the consequent satisfaction convinces the one who prays of the reality of the transaction and of the value of the virtue of faith.

More often, the painful experiences continue, and then the prayer life undertakes to transform these into pleasant experiences, that is to say, into some kind of satisfaction by finding meaning in them. The painful experiences may be seen as purifying or as penance, as reparation, or as preparatory to a positive experience yet to come. This approach can be further elevated to the experience of sharing in the redemptive sufferings of Christ. This perspective on life produces a deep level of satisfaction in the experiencer, even though the surface level of the human life is painful. But in order for this to happen, the experiencer has had to shift the sense of selfhood a bit from the level of the sense-body and the emotional personality to the understanding and believing level of the mind.

Another approach to the prayer life locates our selfhood in the performer of moral acts. This moral-agent self then relates to God in prayer in terms of God's approval or disapproval, in terms of pleasing or displeasing God, in terms of seeking God's aid to do what is morally right. As this prayer life progresses, one discovers many things about oneself. Some people report that they find in the depths of themselves the potentiality for all kinds of evil. Possibly they find also the potentiality for heroic goodness. People become very sensitive to their motives for behaving in certain ways; there seem to be wheels within wheels within wheels, accounting for attitudes, feelings, and actions. Their prayer life tends to be focused on analyzing or seeing into the deeper roots of their motives and seeking—and asking divine aid—to purify these motives. On the constructive side, the one who prays will probably also contemplate and strive to imitate the good motives and good deeds of Christ and the saints, invoking the latter's help in making a good moral-agent self. Here the sense of identity is located more in the person as actor than in the person as receiver of good or bad experiences.

A fourth approach reflects on all the foregoing and draws a metaphysical conclusion: I am nothing; God is everything. I am a creature, a contingent, finite, and flawed being. I can do nothing of myself but sin. The source of all being and all goodness is God alone, who is Another Being; whatever share in being and goodness I have, I have it only as God's gift to me. All I can do is receive.

Now, I wish to make two comments on these modalities of identity and prayer. The first comment is this: If the identity is located as indicated, the prayer life that follows is correct. One who identifies with the pleasures and pain of the flesh and the emotions and who identifies God as the controller of these experiences is bound to appeal to God to control the experiences in the experiencer's favor, even if the satisfaction level has to go from the flesh and the emotions to an interpreted sense of meaningfulness. God may not then give pleasure but meaning, and that is more important.

One who identifies with the moral-agent self acts correctly in contemplating God as exemplar and in using the prayer exercise to purify the moral motives and strengthen the moral virtues. And one who identifies with the finite and contingent being does right to contemplate God as the source of infinite and absolute being. We may also notice that the self-identification always carries with it a corresponding God-identification. The two undergo their transformations together, and I think that the self-identification probably comes first, drawing the God-identification after it as its complement.

The second comment is the difficult one. It suggests that all of these modes of prayer have in common an unquestioned concept of the nature and location of the self that is not necessary and may not be the best we can do. If we change it, let us look for the sort of thing to happen that happened in the other examples. That is, we will not switch from the affirmation in our assumption to its negation, but we will reframe the whole outlook so that both of those views will be seen to be inadequate or inapplicable.

All the above modes of prayer assume without question that the identity of the one who prays is in the finite order. Let us see what this implies. To be finite means to be a determinate being, one with particular qualities or predicates, one capable of description. It is to be *this* rather than *that*, to have

one's being limited by what one is not. "All determination is by negation," the logicians say, and this
is true. The chair is not the table. I am not you—as
long as we think this way. In fact, my very being
"I" is dependent on my not being "you." This is our
cherished individuality, our unique personality, our
inalienable responsibility for our own moral acts
which merit praise or blame, and so on.

But please notice, it is precisely this location of
our identity that produces the experiences of pleasure and pain, the involutions of moral motivation,
and ultimately the sense of metaphysical impotence.
A self that identifies itself by excluding and negat-
ing other beings—that defines itself by saying "I
am I insofar as I am not you"—necessarily must
defend its finite being against the competitive presence of all other finite beings. All other beings must
be dealt with in some way so that they enhance, or
at least protect, one's own being and do not harm
it. One must either destroy them, or convert them
to one's own use, or possibly arrange to live in a
subordinate and dependent position relative to a
stronger being. Very rarely one may work out a
fairly equal symbiotic relation of interdependence.
All relations are relations of "having," as distinguished from "being," beginning with "having"
existence, and these relations are important to the
self for maintaining it in existence and making its
life worthwhile.

Now, it may be that this perception and identification of the self as defined by mutual negation,
as obliged to defend itself in relation to all other
beings, is in error. This is what it is to walk away
from the mirror and forget our natural face. We take
on instead a set of artificial faces. We present ourselves to the world under our various titles, our roles,
our functions, our relations. We have only to make
a quick test, asking ourselves to answer the question
"Who are you?" to see that our spontaneous way of
identifying ourselves is in terms of these categories
and classes of descriptions.

I should say here clearly that these relations, roles,
and functions are real and true. And the need to
define them by mutual negation and to defend them
by various arrangements of subordination or dependence is correct. As functions or aspects or levels of
our life in the world, this is unavoidable. The question is whether the spiritual self should settle its identity-location in any of them, whether the very heart
of selfhood should find itself there. The suggestion is
that when it does so settle, locate, and identify itself,
it mistakes one of its functional or artificial faces for
its natural face.

The business of the spiritual life is to remember
and return to identifying with our natural face. This
can be done, the Epistle of Saint James says, by looking into the perfect law of liberty. Then, restored to
identity with our natural face, we will be able to be

doers of the Word and not hearers only. If we are hearers only, it is because we identify our ultimate selfhood with the finitude of the artificial faces, their contingency and fragility and our consequent anxiety about them or passivity with respect to the powers that do maintain them.

III

If we are to follow up on the teaching that the work of the spiritual life is the recovery of our natural face as preparation for the doing of the Word, then a quite different type of prayer must be practiced. All the modes of prayer that I described earlier accepted the notion that the descriptive self is the true self, and they proceeded to operate in prayer on this basis. Now we are entertaining the suggestion that the real work of prayer is just to *get rid of* the very assumption that was the foundation of all these other modes of prayer.

It is a matter of shifting the location of the sense of identity. We have to accept the idea that the word *I* does not have a fixed and clear and obvious referent. This is where the transformation that we undergo becomes more and more radical with each breakthrough or illumination. What happens at each stage is that the meaning of the word "I" changes. At least, this is one way of putting it.

It is instructive, I believe, in this connection to notice the various utterances attributed to Jesus in the Gospels, ranging in a spectrum from "Why do you call me good? No one is good but God," through "I do nothing of myself, but the Father dwelling in me performs his works" and "I do as the Father commands me," or "I do what I see the Father doing," up to the final "The Father and I are one; whoever sees me sees the Father." The referents of the word "I" in these speeches are not the same. This is the point we have to grasp and to apply to ourselves.

This is a difficult point to grasp, probably because we are so accustomed to the notion of a fixed meaning for the word "I" and also because our whole language system is set up on the assumption that the world is composed of a multitude of separate substances, hard bounded beings, different and distinct from one another.

I have suggested the image of a spectrum, at one end of which the self says, "I am very different from God." In the middle the self says, "I do nothing, but God is in me, doing." A little later it says, "I also do things, but only by obeying God or by imitating what God does." Only at the other extreme of the spectrum does the self say, "God and I are not different; it doesn't make sense to ask to see God as distinct from seeing me; we can't be separated that way." In this image we may suppose the spectrum itself to remain steady, laid out like a slide rule on a desk. But then the little magnifying lens, through which one focuses on the reading, moves from one end of the scale to the other. This moving lens is the sense of identity.

I want to be clear that the positions on the rule itself do not change. The level of reality that cannot claim goodness for itself is still there and still unable to claim goodness for itself. The level that is an instrument for divine activity remains, and remains an instrument. The level that acts, but acts under obedience or under guidance from above, is also in place and maintains its own way of acting. None of these changes as the lens slips along the rule and goes up to the affirmation "The Father and I are one."

What changes is the referent of the word "I," that is, the level at which the self locates its ultimate identity. If at any time the sense of identity slips down the scale to the level of obedience or instrumentality, then the statements made at those levels are again correct. If that is where your "I" is, then those are the proper things for it to say.

The mistake that we want to avoid—according to the argument that I am making—is to assume that "I" refers to just one referent and then to debate which of the above statements is the correct one: Should we say "I do nothing for myself" or say "Who sees me sees the Father?" This debate drops out of the picture as soon as we give up the assumption that the sense of identity is fixed, that "I" always means the same.

In order to explain this more clearly and to try to describe a possible alternative to the static "I" model, let us now go back to the recommendation in the text from Saint James that we "look into" the "perfect law...of liberty." In "The Living One,"[3] I tried to convey a sense of the self as a present-into-future living being, as a kind of energy or creative process. It is not to be restricted to its past, which is its descriptions. All that is "dead." As living, it is in the act of creating the future from moment to moment. But if this living one is not to be identified with the descriptions of its past, then it must be a self that transcends all these descriptions, and that comes to a realization of itself as transcending all the descriptions by practicing the *via negativa* of denying its identification with these limited selves. I take this to be the metaphysical/mystical meaning of "self-denial."

As it looses itself from identification with each of these bonds—the attachments of the body and its passions, the cravings and griefs of the emotional nature, the localization of the self by its relations, roles, and history, its memberships and allegiances, even its taxonomic position according to biology and various schemes of metaphysics—as it "loses" each of these "selves," the praying consciousness "finds itself" more and more at liberty. The more you take off bondage, the freer you become; the more you lose restrictions, the vaster you become. The more you empty yourself of predicates, the more you become full of Being.

When you are perfectly empty of all predicates—including the description of yourself as a "receiver"—then you are intensely full of pure "I am." And just as this point is reached, it explodes into the creative outpouring energy, "May all of you be and be abundantly!" I do not say this as a theoretical theological or philosophical thesis. I report it as an experience of discovery, and I believe that if you will follow the same path of interior seeking, you will experience it in the same way. You simply persevere in the act of "looking into" the law or principle that makes for perfect liberty until this creative energy bursts forth at the point where all the lines going back into the center of the self converge.

This is the point at which God is closer to you than "you"—meaning your descriptions—are to yourself, as Saint Augustine said. God irrupts in the center of your being, as that fountain of living water that makes you to be. But since God cannot be objectified, cannot be experienced as an object, you have to experience this from the subject side, as if it is your own self-being.

I call this energy irruption *spondic* because it pours out like a sacred libation, and this perfect liberty I call "creative freedom" because it creates what it loves instead of merely responding to it. Just as the transcendent self does not identify itself with its past, so it does not love other beings for their pasts—whether attractive to it or the reverse. The spondic energy that pours out in creative freedom is *agape*, the love that moves to the next moment of the beloved's life, with the will that all shall be good for the beloved. It pours itself as living energy into the beloved as a will to good and abundant being for the beloved, and it takes up its residence there. This living self identifies itself not by its descriptions, which are all ways of saying "I am I by virtue of being unlike you," but it identifies itself by saying to the beloved, "I am in you and you are in me."

This living self says to all other selves, who are beloveds to it, "Take my life as your food; nourish yourselves by my energies; assimilate my very self-hood so that we may be intermingled." In fact, it says to the beloved, "You and I are one; whoever sees me, sees you and whoever sees you, sees me. Whatever anyone does to you, they do to me; what they do to me, they do to you; what you do, I do; and what I do, you do" (cf. John 14:9, Matt. 25:40, John 15:20, Matt. 18:18–20, John 14:12). This, in my view, is the metaphysical and mystical meaning of Holy Communion and the central teaching of the sacramental events and discourse at the Last Supper. It is the casting, like fire on the Earth, of the *agape*, which Christian teaching says is the nature of God, and which is the Source that creates the world.

IV

Since the purpose of the spiritual life, according to most traditions, is that we are to enter into union with the Divine Source and Creative Act, or to realize our eternal union with it, we can understand why the work of prayer could be said to be a matter of learning that our "natural face" is this transcendent self that exercises creative freedom by radiating love to all beings. It is the progress toward the realization of this "natural face" in ourselves, and the finding of it as transcendent and radiant and mutually indwelt by and indwelling the Divine Transcendence and Creative Radiance, that marks out the series of ever more radical transformations in our sense of identity that we undergo in the life of prayer.

The first task, clearly, is to detach the sense of identity from the descriptions, from the artificial faces. This does not mean to find *another* description of yourself which would be the correct one. It means to realize that there is *no* description of *you*. That which is called by your name—your body, your history, your personality, your feelings—none of that is ultimately "you." Whatever is capable of being described and distinguished from other descriptions, all that is to be stripped off so that the remaining selfhood may be called "naked," as it often is called in mystical literature.

All the ascetical practices recommended to us by the various traditions are designed to produce this effect, that we will stop identifying with our descriptions. This is the meaning of "detachment." Notice that this sense of identity is an internal sense of location or perspective, not a way of standing outside ourselves and looking back on ourselves. It is like knowing where you are by your sense of gravity or sense of posture, or the point of view from which you see. You are to coincide with the subjective act of being conscious, not to reflect on the fact of your being or of your being conscious.

You learn it by a kind of practice, as you learn to balance yourself in walking or bicycle riding or swimming. You learn it as you learn to move one muscle without moving the one next to it, as in dancing or playing a musical instrument. You learn it as you learn, under biofeedback training, to produce alpha waves in your brain or to lower your blood pressure. It is a certain subtle sense of where you are or how you are, inside. You may "get the hang of it" suddenly or gradually.

One practice that may be especially important to mention is that all the "pairs of opposites" are to be recognized and treated as polarities of the same limited levels of being. Both pleasure and pain are to be regarded with the same detachment, because they are polarities of the identity sense, "I am the body." Both elation at being praised or being successful and dejection at failure or being reproached or insulted are to be regarded with the same detachment, because they are polarities of the identity sense, "I am my feelings and my personality."

Therefore, in prayer, we are not to blame and berate ourselves, we are not to indulge in feeling guilty, any more than we are to commend ourselves and indulge in feeling complacent, because both indulgences are the same mistake. The mistake is not in our judgment, that we accounted ourselves virtuous when we should have acknowledged some deeper deficiency. The mistake is in identifying ourselves with a level of selfhood on which these feelings make any sense at all, either way.

Now, go back and notice something so there is no misunderstanding. The body will continue to experience pleasure and pain and we will continue to try to keep it in neutral as far as we can. The emotional personality will probably continue to vibrate to kind or unkind words and actions, and we will try to pacify it. We will most likely continue to make mistakes and maybe occasionally commit moral wrongs until we have thoroughly learned the new way. And obviously we must exert ourselves to correct and try to prevent these things. These levels of our being do not drop out of existence as we seek to shift our sense of identity. And we do not drop our responsibility for trying to bring them into their respective beneficial orders, each on its own level.

As we progress, we will not take our pleasures and pains so seriously. Therefore the desires and the sufferings attached to them will diminish. When we do not so much identify with our descriptive selves, we will not have the perceptions and motives that otherwise lead us into moral faults. So those will disappear. But we should not count the improvement on these levels as the achievement of our spiritual goal. From one point of view these improvements are preliminaries to real spiritual attainment, and from another point of view, they are byproducts of it. They are not, however, the main focus. Therefore, the work of prayer is not to seek these improvements directly but to seek to shift our sense of identity away from the whole type of self-concept that underlies both the undesirable and the desirable experiences—since they are always polarities of the same level of being. And this self-concept is the descriptive self. The descriptive being will still be there; it is not unreal. And we lose none of our responsibility for keeping it in right order. But we do not believe that we *are* it, we do not experience ourselves as being located there; we do not perceive life as if we are looking out from that point of view. And just because we do not identify ourselves with the descriptive being, we will be in a much better position to regulate it, to bring it into the natural harmony in which it should operate.

How do we go about trying to shift our sense of identity? There are two ways: prayer or meditation or contemplation, and the actions of everyday life. I have already mentioned the ascetical practices, which are supposed to help us to see through our mistaken identification of ourselves with the levels of bodily and emotional experience. And I have mentioned that prayer should not be a matter of moral evaluation of our lives. Moral reflection is a good thing and should be done, but it is not *per se* a spiritual practice and should not be confused with the proper work of prayer. The proper work of prayer is an effort to experience ourselves being "I" without being any of the descriptions.

There are, of course, many ways of approaching prayer in practice. I will describe only two. One is a way I think I will call the *"hodos* method." In the Gospel according to John, Jesus says, "I am the way, and the truth, and the life" (14:6). The word for "way" is *hodos* ("road"). As I have experienced it, it means that Jesus himself becomes a road or a passage. It seems to work like this: One begins with an ordinary meditation on almost any Gospel event. You can watch it as an outsider until it becomes vivid, and then enter into it as one of the characters in the scene. It is especially helpful to enter into the role of someone who is interacting with Jesus. In this practice, the prayer gradually shifts from discursive to non-discursive as one finally settles on the chief focus of the event and holds that bit steadily before one.

I like to use as an example of this prayer the story of the leper who presented himself before Jesus with the declaration, "You only have to will it, and you can make me clean." Jesus touched him and said, "I do will it: Be clean" (Matt. 8:2–3, RSV). The one who meditates on this event becomes the leper and experiences the interaction with Jesus. You first experience the conviction of the leper that the will of Jesus can heal; then you feel the touch of Jesus' hand and hear his words. At this point the scene holds, and the words are repeated again and again.

What may then happen is that you will find that, by repeating the words over and over, you have slipped out of being the leper and are being Jesus. This is a startling and powerful experience, because now you look out on the world through his eyes, see the leper before you, and feel the enormous power of Jesus' will to heal flowing through you, out to that person.

In this experience you may begin to realize that what you had thought of as different identities have all telescoped, but can be traced back, as if you are tracking a stream to its source. There is the human personality of Jesus and his natural concern for a fellow being. But inside this is the vast will of the Incarnate Divine Word through whom all creation takes place. This will seems to blow through, or shine through, or pour through, or beam through, the human personality like a giant laser. And even inside or behind this is the absolutely invisible Source of being itself.

In the meditator's position of identification with Jesus in this scene, all these experiences have to pass *through* the one who prays. They have to be experienced from the inside, not regarded, however worshipfully, from the outside. As the layers of identity in Jesus reveal themselves, deeper and deeper, the meditator's sense of identity has to shift with them, carried by the prayer. The reality of Jesus thus acts as a passage or a road from the phenomenal world of descriptive being back into the heart of the Godhead. The meditator can begin with any experience in the life of Jesus, and by entering into Jesus' sense of his own identity, beginning from his action or his words and passing to his intention and his feeling, and so back into his sense of selfhood, come into the experience of union with God.

Another way of praying that is being talked about now is called "centering." There are variations on this, too, so I will give you my version. One attempts in this prayer to situate one's sense of spiritual gravity at the very center of one's being, at the point which cannot be described by any predicates, which therefore literally cannot be conceived because no concept is adequate to it. In this sense it cannot be "known" or be "thought." One approaches it rather by "unknowing." But you can be conscious in it because it is the source of consciousness. You do not become un-self-conscious in the sense of becoming unconscious or unaware of being conscious. But you stop looking at what you call "yourself" as if it were an object, as if you could "look" at it. You can only coincide consciously with it. All the sense of con-sciousness pulls in, as it were, and concentrates itself on the focal point of self-being at the center of the soul.

If this is done correctly, it is something like a solar eclipse. All the ordinary lights that we are used to are gradually blotted out until it seems that every-thing that we had known to be ourself is gone. And just as everything is disappearing into this darkness, the crown of light, the corona, bursts forth with breathtaking beauty. Just at the moment when we concentrate ourselves in the purity of the sheer zero of spiritual emptiness, it explodes into the cosmic radiance of love.

In this discovery of one's original, natural face, the true self at the center of one's descriptive being, one realizes union with God, who is Original *Agape*. One's being is united with God's being, which is the eternal and continuous act of creative freedom, willing abundant being to all. And thus one's will is united with God's will, as being the same kind of will and the same act of will, a creative freedom that enters into all beings and dwells with them,

projecting spiritual energies toward and into them
that they also may be creative beings.

V

It may be that here a very curious thing happens.
The whole sense of what identity itself means comes
into question. Not only does the sense of identity
shift from what I have called the artificial faces, or
the descriptive levels of being, to the natural face,
the transcendent self, but it is not clear how to dis-
tinguish this transcendent self from the Divine Being,
because both are undescribable acts of outpouring
love and both find their identity precisely by their
indwelling of what we—from our descriptive point
of view—would call "other" beings.

Saint Teresa of Avila likened her experience of
the divine union to sunlight pouring through two
windows into the same room. Inside the room it is
all one light. I think this is a good image. I was going
to suggest the metaphor of "confluence." I think of
life, or self-being, as a kind of flow or beam of energy.
And *agape*, which is in the spiritual order the means
of identification, is the flowing or beaming of one
stream into another so that the two are then both
two and one.

This is another case of an assumption that must
be abandoned. In the light of what we understand
about the Trinity, we cannot ask ourselves whether
we are "the same as" God or another being, or

whether we are "different from" and "separate from" that other. These are not the right questions; there is no satisfactory way to answer them in either direction. "Identity" or selfhood is not such a being that "same" and "different" can be applied to it. The peculiar thing about it is that if we are to try to use these concepts of "same" and "different" we shall be obliged to affirm them both and still to say that the "sameness" and the "differentness" do not conflict with one another. That is as close as we can get with the categories and the logic derived from material experience. But it is more helpful, in my opinion, to say strongly that these concepts are strictly inapplicable. This alerts us to look for another level of experience.

We are used to thinking of the self—even a self that changes its opinion about, or its experience of, its identity-location—as a single, somehow uniquely identifiable being. But it may not be that simple. If the paradigm of being is the Trinitarian *perichoresis*, the mutual indwelling of the Divine Persons in one another and the production of their unity out of the intensity of their self-giving to one another, as the Greek theology suggests, then we ourselves must also be like this. It may therefore be that all true persons, transcendent selves, sources of creatively free *agape*, are circles whose centers are nowhere and whose circumferences are everywhere. And thus they may all overlap and interpenetrate each other with an intimacy that we can scarcely imagine, because we think of intimacy and maintenance of individual personhood as inversely proportional. But the revelation of the Divine Being may be precisely this, that it extends the intimacy of its interior life to all of us and that in fact this is the only way in which it is *possible* for a spiritual being to exist. This may be what the mystery of the Trinity is meant to tell us.

The whole question of unique "identity" *at all*— the identity that is "mine" or "yours"—may disappear because "my" identity is "your" identity is "Christ's" identity, is God's identity. There is an "I," but it is not the "I" that had formerly been meant when "I" was said; rather, where "I" is said, one could now as well say "Christ" (cf. Gal. 2:20). And finally, God is all in all (1 Cor. 15:28).

Some utterances in spiritual literature cannot be understood except from the point of view of the experience that gave rise to the utterance in the first place. Outside that experience, these sayings appear incorrect or arrogant or oversimplified, as if proper account had not been taken of the structure of the world. And indeed, if one says "I" meaning the descriptive being, then the statements made by mystics are incorrect. They only become correct when attributed to the realm of the transcendent self, in which such intermingling and confluence of identities is possible and perhaps necessary.

In conclusion, let me just point to a last idea deriving from that passage from James. As the prayer life reaches some degree of realization in the course of this looking into the law of liberty, the meditator begins to be able to be a doer of the Word and not merely a hearer. One begins to be able really to love all other beings as one's self. This is simply not possible before one remembers and identifies with one's "natural face," the central self in which God's *agape* is the source of life. But the closer one approaches to this realization, this transformation in the sense of identity, the more one will be able actually to do the divine act of radiating being and love-energy to all beings of the world.

This is when "spiritual life" in the true sense begins. All this work of prayer in order to reach that point was not really "spiritual life," although we call it that because it is concerned with the spiritual life. It is only after we have "looked into"—gazed upon and grasped—"the perfect law, the law of liberty," and after we have "persevered," that we become not hearers who forget but doers who act, and then we are blessed in our doing. [4]

❉

COMMENTARY

On Section I

"The work of prayer is to transform our sense of identity" (p. 84). Bruteau's powerful opening statement may be initially unsettling to those more accustomed to thinking of prayer as "*to* God, *on behalf of* others." Whatever became of prayer as "praise and petition"?

But her point is really more subtle—and not far removed, I believe, from the same point Jesus was making when he said, "The one who wishes to save his life will lose it, and the one willing to lose it will find it." This losing and finding is what Bruteau is speaking of. The transformation she has in mind is the fundamental liberation of our sense of identity from a selfhood too exterior, rigid, and time-bound into an interior spaciousness that can "travel at the speed of love." To use an analogy from modern physics, she is encouraging us to experience our basic selfhood in wave rather than particle form: not as a fixed, nucleated entity, but as a flowing stream of relationality and coherence (which she will later call "spondic energy").

The reason for undergoing this transformation is not personal self-realization or even the personal experience of "transforming union," but to be able to participate fully here and now in the generative, kenotic energy of the Trinity, which makes itself fully manifest in the act of giving itself away. Nucleated selfhoods cannot do that. The human in particle form is inherently unstable, anxiety-ridden, and prone to judgment (even violence) when it senses itself threatened. Only as we become free of this limited, "stuck" definition of ourself can we flow into one another and into life in true Gospel fashion, loving our neighbor as ourself (not *as much as* ourself, as the limited mind will always unconsciously append).

She grounds the scriptural basis of her assertion in the epistle of James (1:23–25), specifically in its injunctions against being merely "a hearer of the word and not a doer." James is not usually considered one of the soaring mystical visionaries of the church. His solidly "yang" teachings around faith and works are not generally favored in the ethereal halls of contemplative *lectio divina*. But whether she turns James end-for-end or merely elicits the deeper meaning that was there all along, she takes him far beyond his usual range of interpretation. Without altering a word, she uses this passage to suggest that only through undergoing this series of inner transformations—"remembering our natural face," as James puts it—can we actually *become* doers of the Word. Her explanation follows the classic trajectory of Wisdom teaching that we fall into forgetfulness, losing sight of our true face in a maze of artificial constructs and compounding the problem (like the

Pharisees in John 9) by thinking that we already see. The transformation she has in mind is one of *awakening*. And this, as we will shortly see, entails not just a moral *metanoia* ("Change the direction in which you're looking for happiness!" as Thomas Keating so emphatically puts it), but a perceptual one as well: "Go beyond the mind! Go into the larger mind!" [5] More than anything else, awakening is an increasing ability to recognize and transcend the suppositions that frame our basic perceptual field—or in other words, to be able to look *at* the filter that heretofore we have only looked through.

On Section II

In this second section Bruteau gets down to the meat of her argument. She introduces two highly original and challenging ideas, both of them potentially revolutionary in their impact.

The first, on pages 89–92, is her insight that how a person prays—that is, what kind of prayers he or she addresses to God—is an inescapable function of where that person is carrying his or her sense of selfhood. Prayer and identity are joined at the hip; as you conceive of your identity (probably unconsciously), so you will pray. And as those prayers "rise like incense before God," they carry with them the unmistakable, telltale signs of the sense of identity out of which they emerge.

She illustrates this point with several examples. If your sense of identity is located in the experience (or more precisely, the experien*cer*) of pain and pleasure—as is typically true of egoically based selfhood—then your prayer will tend to be some variation on the basic theme of "O God, take away my painful experiences and give me pleasurable ones," or its more sophisticated nuancing, "O God, at least make my painful experiences meaningful." Alternatively, if you experience yourself as a moral agent (and God as the judge), your prayer will be for assistance in conducting yourself rightly. If you experience yourself as metaphysically impotent ("contingent, frail, and finite," as Bruteau puts it), your prayers will tend in the direction of "I can do nothing but receive your grace."

She is quick to point out that insofar as our self-identification is located as indicated, the prayer that flows from it is valid. And hence, it is really futile to argue (as so often happens in seminary classes and inter/intradenominational warfare) over the validity and efficacy of one form of prayer as opposed to another. Is prayer of petition more valid (advanced, Christian, efficacious, etc.) than, say, contemplative prayer? That is not the point. The real point of contact is not in the form of the prayer itself but in the identity of the one who prays, because here, as we shall see, is where the radical transformative power of prayer is actually lodged.

From this platform Bruteau then goes on to make her most challenging leap. Have you noticed, she asks, that all of the above-mentioned identities locate the sense of selfhood in the *finite* order? She is not only speaking metaphysically here; she is also putting on her hat as mathematician and logician to give you a "formal/logical" definition of finite. To be finite means to be a "determinate being," which in turn means "one with particular qualities or predicates.... It is to be *this* rather than *that*, to have one's being limited by what one is not. 'All determination is by negation,' the logicians say, and this is true. The chair is not the table. I am not you—as long as we think this way" (pp. 92–93).

Clearly, Bruteau is naming here the primary filter through which we post-Cartesian Westerners look upon ourselves and the world. It sets in early and cuts deep: I hear my three-year-old granddaughter singing along with the "Sesame Street" jingle, "One of these things is not like the other ..." and realize that, as she learns how a cat is not a dog, she is also absorbing the basic methodology of mental/egoic consciousness: perception through differentiation.[6] Little does she (or any one of us) know that in a short—terrifyingly short—time, she will come to view the world, herself, and all others through this useful but ruthlessly isolating binary shorthand. She will come to anchor her uniqueness (and hence her "specialness" before God) in what makes her different from everyone else rather than in what makes her *one* with everyone else (which is what the word "unique" actually means). And in this location of her identity, she will inevitably experience herself in competition and potential conflict with other human beings, struggling to defend her "uniqueness" against all other competing uniquenesses. Welcome to the Fall! Bruteau ironically points out that it is this initial mistake of identifying our selfhood with our finite descriptors (our "predicates," as she calls them) that gives rise to those experiences of pain, alienation, and guilt which fuel the usual modalities of our prayer life. These are the "artificial faces," created not so much by sin as by the basic perceptual tool we use to navigate reality: our mental/egoic "operating system." Programmed to differentiation as its fundamental interpretive mode, it is unable to perceive or sustain unitive oneness.

Bruteau's insight in this one paragraph has been foundational to my experience of centering prayer. In twenty years of journeying with this prayer form, I have discovered more and more strongly how its most enduring gift is gradually to "rewire" a person from mental/egoic perception (with its inevitably nucleated and finite sense of selfhood) into something more spacious and unboundaried.[7] In *Centering Prayer and Inner Awakening*, I have identified this alternative operating system as "heart perception," and described it from reference points within the classic Wisdom traditions of the West.[8] But the core insight came to me from Bruteau more than two decades ago.

On Section III

This next session—the heart of her essay—rests on a metaphor to which the familiar adage applies: if you can accurately identify the object she is describing and can remember having used it yourself, you are officially *old*! It is the slide-rule on that pencil box that you lugged along with you during your grade school years. But whether you can relate to her image or not, she is using it to make the point that our sense of identity is fluid; it does not always come from the same place inwardly. This was true even for Jesus. His "Why do you call me good? No one is good except the Father" does not come from the same place as "I and the Father are one." The former reveals a more constricted and contingent sense of selfhood; the latter is totally unboundaried. In the same way, our own locus of identity is constantly fluctuating back and forth along a continuum from constricted to unboundaried, and back again. Sometimes the fluctuations are virtually instantaneous!

Practitioners of centering prayer, particularly those experienced in Thomas Keating's teachings on the "False Self System" and "The Divine Therapy," will already have a wide range of personal experience in these varying degrees of constriction and interior freedom. At the extreme left of our "identity slide rule," in its most constricted position, is the false-self system: totally at the mercy of its "emotional programs for happiness," responding to the world out of its instinctual needs and reactivity. Those first life-changing breakthroughs in centering prayer occur as the practitioner learns, through the faithful practice of this prayer, to shift this "moving lens of identity" a notch to the right, into what I elsewhere term "high egoic functioning." At this point the person feels a release, sometimes ecstatically so, from the constriction of the false-self system. But the search for the true self is still being conducted, in Bruteau's terminology, "within the finite order." From this vantage point, finding one's true self appears to be a project of finding the *right* description of oneself, the correct set of descriptors to convey the uniqueness that one truly is. "I used to be a corporate control freak, but now I see that I'm really sort of a mystic …," and so forth.

It will be the goal of the rest of her essay to demonstrate how this particular resting place in the quest for a true self-identity does not push far enough. The goal is not to find the right description but to get rid of descriptions altogether! "If this living one is not to be identified with the descriptions of its past," she writes (p. 98), "then it must be a self that transcends all these descriptions and comes to a realization of itself as transcending all the descriptions by practicing the *via negativa* of denying its identification with these limited selves." With her characteristic irony, she adds, "I take this to be the metaphysical/mystical meaning of 'self-denial.' "

Again, those on the contemplative path will have already had significant interior experience of life beyond the descriptors. This is, after all, a nutshell description of centering prayer itself. As all the thoughts, the descriptors, the memories rise during prayer time, one simply lets them go and rests in the unboundaried, undivided fullness. The real question, then, is, *Where does one return that sliding lens of identity when one emerges from the prayer itself?* Most will routinely return it to somewhere around high egoic functioning: a quieting of the programs for happiness, but still a strong sense of the finite self in quest of its "experience" of transforming union. Bruteau will suggest that we can live consciously, creatively, and coherently without recourse to the "finite self" crutch; our lens of identity can come to rest stably and permanently in a selfhood that does not rely on the fatal double-bind of trying to perceive unity through an operating system attuned to differentiation.

"When you are perfectly empty of all predicates— including the description of yourself as a 'receiver'— then you are intensely full of pure 'I am'," she writes

(p. 98). "And just as this point is reached, it explodes into the creative outpouring energy." This spondic energy—the love that moves the sun and the stars pours out as the lifeblood of the communion of saints and the joyous, reckless self-giving of the Gospel path.

On Section IV

In this section Bruteau's attention turns to the practical. She gives us two core spiritual practices to facilitate this transformation of our inner sense of identity—but not before reminding us once again that the goal is not to find the "correct" description of ourself, but to move beyond descriptions altogether. You get the hang of it, she adds, by feel and with practice, like learning to balance a bicycle or swim. "It is a certain subtle sense of where you are or how you are, inside" (p. 102). She emphasizes that this is not a mental process: "You are to coincide with the subjective *act* of being conscious, not reflect on the fact of your being or of your being conscious" (my italics).

The first practice, which she calls "the *hodos* [path] method" (see p. 105), corresponds directly to stage two (*meditatio*) in the practice of *lectio divina*, in which one summons the powers of the faculties (imagination, reason, visualization, emotional empathy) to break open a scriptural passage. In this case, she suggests that we "play-act" the Gospel narratives—and not be reticent to take on the role of Jesus. What better way to "put on the mind of Christ" than to understudy him meticulously, as any good actor labors to get inside the character that he or she is portraying?

The second practice she calls "centering." But remember that this is not centering prayer the way it is now taught and practiced.[9] The essence of centering prayer is a simple letting-go of all thoughts, images, emotions, and energies—even the energy of the gathered "*I am*" presence. In the practice that Bruteau describes, there is an initial intentional effort to "draw into" the center of one's very being, withdrawing all subject/object wanderings of the mind, and simply sit in the spondic energy coiled at the core of one's being—"quivering like a bead of mercury," in Rumi's powerful image.

I must confess that I stumbled onto this practice—and the subsequent "solar eclipse" and "explosion" that she describes on page 108—totally by accident back in the early 1980s in my own attempts to learn centering prayer. Having come from strictly concentrative methods of meditation, centering prayer bedeviled me with its lack of instructions as to where to place my attention. I could not conceive of a meditation method without "single-point concentration." "Don't put your attention *anywhere*!" Father Keating kept repeating, but I just could not see how that would work. Finally, in sheer frustration as I sat down on my prayer mat one afternoon, I decided to put my attention on "the whole of my yearning for God." Unbeknownst to me, this was an exact replication of the route to direct center that Bruteau describes, and the subsequent explosion of energy inside nearly knocked me off my mat! While I eventually got the hang of centering prayer, I have never forgotten that incident and continue to marvel at the sheer nuclear force of that "I am" energy coiled inside each one of us, if we could only set it free!

ON SECTION V

Bruteau is evidently thinking in just these terms. Her final section is a beautiful prose poem describing transformed life once that "particle" sense of selfhood has learned how to flow as wave—or in other words, when non-dual consciousness has become the stable seat of one's identity. Her vision is formed in the core Trinitarian notion of *perichoresis* (literally, "the dance around"): one beingness flowing into another in total self-giving love, and in that very dance making manifest what Love is like. "It may be, therefore, that all true persons…are circles whose centers are nowhere and whose circumferences are everywhere," she ponders (pp. 110–111)—"And thus, they may all overlap and interpenetrate with an intimacy we can scarcely imagine." These may be challenging words to those accustomed to the egoic world with its strong sense of "maintaining healthy boundaries." But it captures in a powerful way the original vision of the communion of saints, the mystical Body of Christ, and provides an authentically Christian expression of the new collectivity to which our planet seems to be being called. These are challenging words into which we can and must grow.

CLOSING REMARKS

In conclusion I would have to say that I do not *fully* buy the implication of her paradigm: that the goal is to move the lens of identity permanently and as quickly as possible in the direction of total interior freedom. There's too much Vedanta speaking here. What most interests me is how all of us as human beings contain within ourselves the full range of self-identity, from most constricted to utterly infinite—and that our lives fluctuate back and forth along this spectrum. For me, that is the real point: not to prefer one end of the spectrum to the other, but to fluctuate *consciously*! Perhaps like Jesus, we all have two natures within us, fully divine and fully human, and the real "hinge of salvation" runs through our awkward but spiritually priceless efforts to weave them together.

At any rate, what seems most important not to lose sight of, as we embrace the marvelous spaciousness of Bruteau's paradigm, is that at all stages and "levels" of prayer God is equally and fully present. The prayer of an alcoholic hitting rock bottom is no less "advanced" or efficacious than the meditator on her mat experiencing the fullness of the spondic energy. In fact, part of the art of prayer as we grow as human beings is to learn which sense of self-identity is most authentic to the situation that we are experiencing. A close friend of mine, a Presbyterian-turned-Buddhist, who came through some very serious health issues this past year, confessed to me that the breakthrough moment in his struggle came when he finally realized that what he needed to do was not to dissolve all fears into passing temporal phenomena but to kneel beside his bed and pray, "Lord, Jesus, help me!" The Divine loves us across the full range of our being, and as we travel "toward" our vision of oneness, whatever that may be, we must never forget that *we are already there* in the complete fullness of the heart of God, because God is as present in two-ness as in oneness, being author of them both.

Chapter 5

READING LIVING WATER:
*The Integral Place of
Contemplative Prayer
in Christian Transformation*

David G. R. Keller

> *We shall never rest, until we become that
> which, in God, we have always been.*
> — MEISTER ECKHART

PART ONE:
A RATIONALE FOR HUMAN TRANSFORMATION
AND CONTEMPLATIVE PRAYER:
THE NEED FOR TRANSFORMATION

> *Why are the nations in an uproar? Why do
> the peoples mutter empty threats?*[1]

IDENTITY AND COMMUNITY are fundamental components of human society. When they become endangered or unclear, the threads that form the fabric of society begin to fray. No one can deny that the international fabric of our world is wearing thin. Frantic efforts to establish or preserve individual and national identities are producing many of the personal and societal addictions present in modern societies: drugs, materialism, personal advancement, fail-safe security, nationalism, extreme partisanship, and ever-expanding progress and competition for resources. These addictions share responsibility for much of the conflicts, power struggles, hegemony, violence, and injustices present between and within nations and religious traditions. It is ironic that our legitimate need for identity and community often prompt widespread use of military, economic, political, and religious coercion. At a deeper level lie three insidious weapons of mass destruction that are often used to help establish identity and preserve community: self-centeredness, self-assertion, and self-interest. This is true for nations, religions, and individuals. Yet, this bleak situation will not erase the goodness of creation or the sanctity of human life. It will not eliminate the influence of millions of caring and compassionate people throughout the world who risk serving their neighbors. It will not dilute the rich and diverse cultural and technological creativity and innovative spirit of humankind. At the same time, many consequences of our obsessive and self-serving efforts to establish identity and community have their origin in a spiritual amnesia that is a source of destructive human evil. We are in danger of de-sacralizing human life and losing sight of what is most fundamental about life itself. What direction should we take and what can we do? Perhaps we should begin by looking beyond ourselves and beyond "doing."

> Who has gauged the waters in the palm of [God's] hand, or with its span set limits to the heavens? Who has held all the soil of the Earth in a bushel, or weighed the mountains on a balance and the hills on a pair of scales? Who has set limits to the spirit of the Lord? (Isa. 40:12–13a, NEB)

Wendell Berry, an American writer, farmer, and social critic points out a fundamental societal problem: "It is impossible to prefigure the salvation of the world in the same language by which the world has been dismembered and defaced."[2] It is not easy to recognize our limitations and even harder to accept our errors. Raimon Panikkar, philosopher and leader in interreligious dialogue, reminds us to be honest about ourselves: "It is the nature of human experience to know that human experience is limited, not only in a linear segment by the future but also by its composition, by the very foundation that is given to it."[3]

Václav Havel, the former president of the Czech Republic, poet, playwright, and social critic, has exhorted world leaders to be open to a "change of consciousness." Havel believes that over-reliance on military, economic, and institutional resources will never produce lasting solutions to the challenges we face today. We must change the way we see each other and the world. [4]

A change of consciousness will require a transformation of self (a new identity) that will lead toward a transformed vision of other people and the world (a new awareness of community). This will not happen overnight, nor is it one more task for us to accomplish for ourselves and the good of the world. This kind of transformation begins with listening, requires a letting-go of control of the outcome, and takes place within each individual. It will be difficult because conventional wisdom has taught us to be suspicious of anything we cannot define or control. It is a Catch-22 situation. We have created a world we cannot fix because it is a world of our own creation. But deep inside us is a longing for what our spirits know is authentic human life. How can we experience what already lies within us?

Dietrich Bonhoeffer, whose writings on community and discipleship are modern classics, believed that the vocation of every person is to discover who we already are. What did he mean? His words affirm the heart of the Judeo-Christian awareness that human beings are created in the image of God and that our vocation is to become fully and authentically human. Our calling is to manifest the image of God in the way we live. This is a journey across the span of years and variety of experiences that form each person's life. It is dynamic spiritual transformation. Bonhoeffer reflects the wisdom of Jesus of Nazareth who said: "I have come that you may have life, and have life in abundance."

Jesus observed that people in his society were not living full and abundant lives. He realized from his own experience that a willingness to "die" to one's self is the beginning of a transformation leading toward abundant (authentic/true) life. Jesus' "gospel" preaching, both in private and in public, called for a change of consciousness that comes with a great price from our point of view: dying to our control of the formation of our own lives. The fourth evangelist has him say to Nicodemus, "Very truly, I tell you, no one can see the kingdom of God without being born from above" (John 3:3). Similarly, in Luke:

> If any want to become my followers, let them deny themselves and take up their cross daily and follow me. For those who want to save their life will lose it, and those who lose their life for my sake will save it. What does it profit them if they gain the whole world, but lose or forfeit themselves? (Luke 9:23–25)

> Do not be afraid, little flock, for it is your Father's good pleasure to *give you the kingdom*. Sell your possessions and give alms. Make purses for yourselves that do not wear out, an unfailing treasure in heaven, where no thief comes near and no moth destroys. For where your treasure is, there your heart will be also." (Luke 12:32–34, my emphasis.)

This is the heart of the Christian path and requires sustained contemplation to experience and embody.

The Need for Contemplation

What is contemplation in the Christian tradition? In response to Jesus' call for personal transformation, contemplative prayer is a grace-filled attentiveness to God that initiates and sustains a change of consciousness, leading to ... love of God and neighbor. This understanding of contemplative prayer ... that Christian contemplation is ... in Holy Scripture, is grounded in personal experience of Christian community, and embraces a variety of practices that sustain our ability, as Saint Paul exhorts us, to "pray always." Contemplative prayer has a constant presence throughout the Bible. [5]

Contemplation, in its variety of forms, is an act of being present to what is most fundamental in life: *God's creative and sustaining presence in every aspect of reality*. Contemplation is an opportunity for the mind and the heart to be joined in that inner place where God is uniquely present to every human being. In that "inner room," as Jesus reminded us, we experience unconditional love and listen to God's desires for ourselves and for the world. This intimate communion reveals our true identity and is the antidote for our spiritual amnesia.

The discipline of contemplative prayer is essential for the transformation of the world because it offers an opportunity for each person who is present and vulnerable to the Holy One *to experience their own transformation.*[6] Contemplation is not only an act of presence; it is a sacrament of awareness and vision. It is the venue for each person's change of consciousness. By emptying ourselves we take the risk of seeing ourselves, the world, and the Holy One through God's eyes. We begin to recognize the unity of all being because the false distinctions that separate us from other people and the natural world are unveiled. When we lose sight of God in our busyness and self-centeredness, we lose sight of what it means to be human. As we are able to see the world through God's eyes, we learn to value the sacredness of life and our personal bond with every aspect of the natural world. This re-discovery of identity and community is a lifelong process of transformation.

The role of contemplation in human transformation has three fundamental manifestations: listening to God, experiencing and being formed by God's presence, and manifesting the presence of God in us through our desires, words, and actions. Listening to and experiencing the Holy One makes human transformation and a change of consciousness possible. Part Three will discuss these three aspects of contemplation in more detail. Part Two

will set the context for the essential role of contemplative prayer in Christian living by exploring
human transformation as the good news of the earliest Christian communities.

PART TWO: TRANSFORMATION
IS THE VOCATION OF EVERY CHRISTIAN

The Center Point of the Earliest Christian Gospel

As we shall see, transformation was the center point
of the earliest Christian faith communities, the patristic period, and the wisdom of the desert mothers and
fathers because it was the heart of the life and teaching of Jesus. The meaning of transformation will
emerge as we explore, briefly, these expressions of
early Christian prayer-filled wisdom, experience, and
preaching. It is important to note that transformation was understood as a *normal process*. It was not
intended for an elite minority. It was proclaimed as
the inheritance of all human beings. Transformation
had (and still has) a two-fold nature:

First, it is the natural unfolding of authentic
human life; it is becoming who we truly are
through the grace of God. Although desire for
and consciousness of the process may begin with
a specific intention and/or "event," it is a lifelong
process that is never complete. It is an eternal
movement forward into our life with God. Without

transformation our lives are incomplete. In this context, transformation is, in the prophet Isaiah's words, a "breaking-in" of our true self to every fiber of our being. This incarnation of the real presence of God in us becomes the source of an energetic and unconditional love of God and our neighbor. We experience a fullness of joy and freedom that Jesus desires for every person: "I have said these things to you so that my joy may be in you, and that your joy may be complete" (John 15:11).

Second, at the same time, transformation can be a *return* to our authentic self (our natural state) after a period or periods of willful desire to be in control of our own lives. This unnatural state of human life rejects God's desires for us in favor of unrestrained self-centeredness, self-reliance, and self-interest. This state of being is sinful and yields evil consequences because it is a rejection of our authentic self and God's loving desires for us. However, transformation is not a movement from an original "evil," material human state to a "good," spiritual form of being. This second aspect of transformation is not separate from the first, but "breaks in" when we become aware of the consequences of our rejection of God's desires. In this context, transformation becomes a "turning toward" God and our true self. Repentance is a powerful and genuine desire to move toward what we rejected. Yet, the image of God, our original and indelible identity, is never lost.

A logical question at this point is: "What does transformed human life look like?" A thorough response is beyond the scope of this chapter. Although transformation is unique for each person, some brief, general comments are necessary. The earliest Christian faith communities looked to the life of Jesus of Nazareth as the manifestation of authentic human life. He is the "exemplar" and source of what we are called to become. The source of his abundant and compassionate living was his openness to and communion with God. The New Testament letters, especially Paul's letters, point to "the fruits of the Spirit" as manifestations of a transformed life. [7]

Transformation in the
Earliest Christian Communities

At the core of the Gospel is the invitation to be changed, made into a new form, and it is the experience of that transformation which gives the writings of the New Testament their power. [8]

Saint Paul describes the process of human transformation in a Christian context in a variety of ways:

- *Being rooted in the fullness of Christ who is the fullness of God in bodily form*: "As you have therefore received Christ Jesus the Lord, *continue to live your lives in him, rooted and built up in him* and established in the faith, just as you were taught, abounding in thanksgiving. See to it that no one takes you captive through philosophy and empty deceit, according to human tradition, according to the elemental spirits of the universe, and not according to Christ. For in him the whole fullness of the deity dwells bodily, *and you have come to fullness in him*, who is the head of every ruler and authority" (Col. 2:6–10, my emphasis).

- *Taking on the mind and behavior of Christ*: "Do nothing from selfish ambition or conceit, but in humility regard others as better than yourselves. Let each of you look not to your own interests, but to the interests of others. *Let the same mind be in you that was in Christ Jesus*, who, though he was in the form of God, did not regard equality with God as something to be exploited, but emptied himself, taking the form of a slave, being born in human likeness" (Phil. 2:3–7, my emphasis). Paul's audacity, both intellectual and spiritual, is difficult to accept as truth and even more difficult to embody. How can a human being "take on" the mind of Christ? Paul's answer is simple. We do not *do* anything except make space for the gift of the grace of God's Spirit: "Now we have received not the spirit of the world, but the Spirit that is from God, so that we may understand the gifts bestowed on us by God. *And we speak of these things in words not taught by human wisdom but taught by the Spirit, interpreting spiritual things to those who are spiritual.* Those who are unspiritual do not receive the gifts of God's Spirit, for they are foolishness to them, and *they are unable to understand them because they are spiritually discerned.* Those who are spiritual discern all things, and they are themselves subject to no one else's scrutiny. 'For who has known the mind of the Lord so as to instruct him?' *But we have the mind of Christ"* (1 Cor. 2:12–16, my emphases). Paul is not speaking of a core of spiritually elite persons. He is speaking of a human change of consciousness available to all persons who accept the gift of personal transformation. Thomas Keating describes this as "moving progressively toward higher, more adequate patterns of thinking and knowing."[9] It is a gift for all, but we each walk the path in a variety of ways and are at different places along the way.

• *Being a dwelling place of Christ that manifests all the fullness of God*: "I pray that, according to the riches of [God's] glory, he may grant that you may be strengthened in your inner being with power through his Spirit, and *that Christ may dwell in your hearts through faith, as you are being rooted and grounded in love.* I pray that you may have the power to comprehend, *with all the saints*, what is the breadth and length and height and depth, and *to know the love of Christ that surpasses knowledge, so that you may be filled with all the fullness of God"* (Eph. 3:16–19, my emphases). Note that Paul emphasizes that this transformed life in Christ is "with all the saints"; it is the *normative Christian life*. In this context Raimon Panikkar states firmly that "Christ-ness" is the core of Christianity, not the institution.

- *Transformation is nothing less than a life that manifests the very life of God* (c.f. Gal. 2:20).

The Second Letter of Peter also proclaims transformation as the primary Christian calling:

His divine power *has given us everything needed for life and godliness*, through the knowledge of him who called us by his own glory and goodness. Thus *he has given us*, through these things, *his precious and very great promises*, so that through them you may escape from the corruption that is in the world because of lust, *and may become participants of the divine nature*." (2 Peter 1:3–4, my emphases)

In this context "corruption" is limitation placed on human life by self-centered and unrestrained passions. The *normal and natural* state of human life is "godliness," made possible by transformation from a self-limiting state to the fullness of human life that "participates" in the "divine nature." This claim is just as audacious as Paul's claims. It is the foundation of the good news of the earliest Christian faith communities and also the core of the teaching and life of the desert fathers and mothers and the patristic period of the early church.

Christian Transformation in the Wisdom and Experience of the Patristic Period

The opening chapter of Genesis asserts that human beings are created in "the image of God" and manifest God's presence in both our finite human existence and in a mysterious, ineffable sacredness. Genesis sets the scene by showing how we, like God, reflect transcendence and immanence in a dynamic tension. Perhaps the Hebrews struggled with these two aspects of God because they experienced a similar struggle within themselves, a struggle common to all human beings. We sense, within us, with an obscure sympathy, a journey in which flesh and blood and human will and being are destined to manifest God's presence. The image yearns to be born. The Hebrew prophets describe how difficult this journey is, how we grow faint and falter along the way, and how God offers to lift us and restore our hope.

Theosis: Moving from Image to Likeness

The early eastern Mediterranean Christian communities of faith viewed this human journey as a movement from bearing the image of God in our nature to *manifesting* the "likeness" of God through our manner of life. Theologians like Basil of Caesarea, Gregory of Nyssa, and Maximos the Confessor, through earnest prayer and study of the Bible, declared to their Greco-Roman culture that the human vocation is to mature from "image" to "likeness," to *participate in and embody* the divine nature.[10] This Christian perspective rejected a common dualistic philosophy of the day, which saw the human and divine natures as separate. The early church fathers insisted that the divine nature in us is not a secret *gnosis* or knowledge. It is not knowledge about God intended to release us from the limitations of finite existence. Patristic theology affirmed experience of God *in the context of human life*. It is here on Earth, within our bodily existence, that we experience and are made whole by divine love. The writings of Gregory and Maximos proclaimed that human beings are sacred and that, while we are not God, we bear the "real presence" of God in time and space. We share God's nature, while remaining God's creatures.

Jesus, the Christ, our Way from Image to Likeness

> I am all at once what Christ is, since he was what I am, and / this Jack, joke, poor potsherd, patch, matchwood, immortal diamond, / is immortal diamond.[11]

Patristic theology affirmed the New Testament proclamation that Jesus of Nazareth is our exemplar because it is the life of God in Jesus that draws

us to incarnate the image of God, already in us, in
our manner of life. The total and absolute congru-
ity of divine transcendence and immanence in Jesus'
life, death, and resurrection make that same union
with God possible for us: "And I, when I am lifted
up from the Earth, will draw all people to myself"
(John 12:32). At the same time, the church fathers
acknowledged the presence of sin in human life. We
have the freedom to reject fullness of life. Sin and
its consequences are the result of a distorted, incomplete humanity. When we reject our divine image,
we also reject being human. Without God there
can be no truly human life. As we have seen, the
fundamental consequence of sin is the denial and
rejection of *authentic humanity* and the pain and
alienation that it produces. Specific consequences of
sin such as greed, injustice, immorality, conflict and
war, and selfish abuse of creation corrupt humanity
through self-love. Sin is a result of the deprivation
of the divine life in us and leads to a personal rejection of grace, the uncreated energies of God. It is a
spiritual form of anorexia. Guilt, in this context, is
an inner reminder of who we really are. Even in the
midst of sin, the image of God remains, and that
blessed truth can reawaken us. A genuine awareness of sin and the seeking of God's forgiveness form
the threshold of transformation. The fundamental
aspect of redemption lies in the restoration of full
humanity in each person. This is the saving power of

the life, death, and resurrection of Jesus. Salvation is the reintegration of each human being to one's true self in Christ. According to Gregory of Nyssa, it is a never-ending process.

Abiding in God: Making Space for Theosis (Transformation)

The theologians of the patristic period placed great emphasis on inner attention to God and manifesting purity of heart. Purity of heart is not a state of moral perfection. It is non-attachment to self, material needs, and even the process of transformation. Purity of heart is an attitude about life formed by God's desires for the world. It is an expansion of the heart that makes moral living flow in us, naturally, through the manifestation of divine love in daily life. The source of moral living becomes love, not legalism. We *desire* congruency with God's will. *Theosis* mirrors in us the Trinitarian life of God through communion with God, who permeates every aspect of our lives. It is a dynamic movement within us of God's transcendence and immanence. In this movement, an incarnation of love, the Spirit of God lures and binds us in *mutual* love. God remains, in essence, totally ineffable, yet the Spirit, by the movement of grace, imparts God's nature and energy to us. The Christ, the Logos, becomes present in us. This is the abundant life Jesus desired for every person and that

Saint Paul experienced when he proclaimed, "It is no longer I who live, but Christ who lives in me" (Gal. 2:20). This grace-filled relationship in each person is the source of the life of the church and mirrors the Trinitarian dimensions of God's being. The church fathers called it "dancing with God."

Dancing with God makes salvation a daily event, as we become more fully human. This means that salvation is a *present reality* and that its potential already lies within us. Sanctification is moving, daily, ever toward God, rather than a static goal or achievement. Jesus said: "The realm of God is already within you." And "It is the Father's good pleasure to give you the kingdom." *Theosis* reflects Paul's awareness that we are called to collaborate with God, in awe and humility, to work out our own salvation. God has given us both the desire and talent that make this possible through the uncreated energy of God in us (Phil. 2:12–13). We do not experience transformation in isolation because we are also formed and nourished in the life of the church. The one who leads us and becomes our life is Jesus, the Christ.

The patristic experience of God and the Christian anthropology that flowed from that experience proclaims that Jesus is "the way, the truth, and the life" because he embodies both the fullness of divine life and authentic human life. Jesus, through his complete openness to the movement of the Spirit, reveals the transcendent essence of the Holy One, whom Jesus called Abba. In *his experience* of this unconditional divine love we glimpse the nature of true humanity. As *we experience* the same love Jesus experienced, it becomes possible for us to see with eyes of love: "Abide in me as I abide in you" (John 15:4). In Christ we are drawn to become what we already are. Like God, we become sources of transformation and life for the world.

Transformation in the Lives and Wisdom of the Desert Fathers and Mothers: Daily Life is the Venue for Transformation

Beginning in the third century, thousands of men and women left the sophisticated and materialistic society of the Roman Empire and went to live in the deserts of Arabia, Egypt, Palestine, and Syria. They wanted a solitude and silence in their search for God that they could not find in the dominant society. In the desert they soon realized that in order to find God a person must know one's self first, and at the same time follow a discipline that enables a person to live for God and other people. They gradually created, through their experience of God and a letting-go of themselves, a prayerful path that unites the head and heart and combines manual labor with work that feeds the soul. Although they chose to live apart from the rest of society, what they learned about themselves through prayer and experience of

God has much to say about what it means to be a human being today. Their wisdom is the heart of the teaching of Jesus and has helped form the Christian path. Their primary source for meditation was the Bible. The legacy of the desert Ammas and Abbas comes to us from collections of sayings and stories, which give a picture of their life in the desert and the wisdom that they learned from it. [12]

The Sacredness of Labor and Daily Life

Our life with God must be seen as a life that accepts the goodness of material life as well as the desire for and goodness of the spiritual life. We offer God our daily living as well as our thoughts, prayers, and spiritual discipline. Our labor provides a spiritual bonding to life and, even though we work for our daily bread, it is the hand of God that supports us. The desert Abbas and Ammas made a distinction between labor (physical work) and praxis (spiritual work). Physical labor contributes to God's creation and makes it possible to have a physical venue in which our spiritual work takes place. Praxis is our work directed toward a purely spiritual purpose. It includes both material and bodily disciplines as well as an inner movement or character that influences our whole being. Praxis results in the "fruit of life," the spiritual vigilance and openness that lead to charity and the formation of our inner life. Labor and praxis are not in competition, but neither should be neglected. There is always the need to integrate the listening and inner growth of praxis with the physical labors that make human life possible. This integration reminds us that our praxis should never be lived at someone else's expense and that our labor should not seek any benefits that go beyond our needs, physical or spiritual.

Labor, woven with praxis, becomes a process in which we learn to make our will congruent with God's will. The "playing-field" of that congruency is our daily labor. As we are able, through praxis, to let go of our ego and the desire to control our life, our labor becomes dedicated to God's desires for the world. Thus, labor may give us the opportunity to be supported by love as God's love becomes embodied in our work.

When labor, as a material reality, is linked through praxis with an interior spiritual reality, the human person experiences *an undivided life* (wholeness of being). If labor is limited to a material reality dominated by the ego, it is separated from God's desires, becomes selfish, and can bring hardship. Labor becomes deeply spiritual, no matter how mundane it may seem, when it becomes an act of self-offering. When labor is released from our control, it becomes *more than what is accomplished*. Such self-giving labor is authentic human work, authentic personhood, and an act of manifesting God's likeness in our lives.

Transformation Manifests
Our Natural State-of-Being

The desert fathers and mothers were painfully and joyously honest about themselves. Their self-knowledge did not come easily, but they realized that it was an indispensable aspect of the humility that makes repentance (and therefore transformation) possible. Their honesty and sorrow for sins were prompted by awareness that they had rejected God's gift of their true self. Abba Dorotheos of Gaza in his *Discourse on Renunciation* said that in sin a person falls "from a state in accord with his nature to a state contrary to nature." Speaking of the transformation in Christ, he says, "For he renewed man in his nature *to what it had been in the beginning*" (my emphasis).[13] This very positive theological anthropology is a central part of the earliest Christian gospel and helps clarify the authentic meaning of transformation.

The Example of Abba Arsenius

Arsenius was one of the most revered rhetoricians and classical scholars of the Roman Empire. He was tutor to the sons of the Emperor Theodosius I and advisor to the emperor. In CE 394 he sensed that, in spite of his influence, luxury, and personal power, his life was incomplete. He prayed, "Lord, what must I do to be saved?" and God's response was, "Flee, be silent, and pray." He left Constantinople and spent fifty-two years as a hermit monk in the Egyptian desert. His withdrawal from conventional society was not a repudiation of culture or politics. The Greek root for the word "saved" in Arsenius's prayer is *soteria*, meaning, literally, to breathe deeply and have abundant health. Arsenius realized that his life at the palace was not full or abundant. He was seeking transformation. The first step was to "flee" or withdraw so that he could begin moving toward wholeness of life. In his case he was fleeing from what he knew was superficial, futile, and scattering. By fleeing he could experience a second step in transformation: listening, in silence. Radical listening, in prayer, exposes the self-reliance, self-interest, and self-centeredness that create a person's false self. Arsenius is an icon of the path to transformation. He remained a teacher, but in the desert the authenticity of his prayer and life became his message rather than his words. Self-reliance, self-centeredness, and self-interest were replaced by humility, charity, and purity of heart.

PART THREE: THE ROLE OF CONTEMPLATIVE PRAYER IN TRANSFORMATION: READING LIVING WATER

What can we learn about contemplation from this brief overview of the central place of transformation in the life and teaching of the early Christian communities? Do the data support my thesis that contemplation has three primary roles in human transformation: (*one*) listening to God, (*two*) experiencing and being formed by God's presence, and (*three*) manifesting the presence of God in our desires, words, and behavior? Another way of saying this is that contemplation helps form us as persons of prayer who are open to constant growth and transformation and seek compassionate relationships and use of creation.

One: Listening to God

Early in my ordained ministry I lived for twelve years among Athabaskan Indians in the Yukon River valley of Alaska. The primary means of travel were dog sleds and small, open boats with outboard engines. A village elder, who had been a riverboat captain, taught me to "read" the water to avoid snags and to stay in the main current: "Pay attention to what you see. Don't just skim the surface. Shortcuts are not always the best way." Contemplative prayer is like that. It is reading the "living water" of life. It keeps us from just skimming the surface and guides us along the main current. The first aspect of listening to God is *paying attention*. The second is *responding to what we hear*. It took me a long time to learn to read the water and take the risk of following where it led. Sometimes my mind drifted or had a better idea, and I would hit a submerged snag or get stuck on a sand bar in shallow water. Listening to God requires disciplined attention, trust, and a faithful response. Its two prerequisites are desire and persistence. We must "show up!"

Contemplative prayer had a major influence in Jesus' transformation. He lived in the midst of political and social unrest and made himself available as teacher, healer, and lover of souls. His days were long and full, and some days "he went home; and the crowd came together again, so that they could not even eat" (Mark 3:20). All four gospels describe his need for and discipline of solitary prayer, especially early in the morning and in the evening. This pattern of quiet listening guided Jesus in the midst of daily situations: "After saying farewell to them, he went up on the mountain to pray." "Once when Jesus was praying alone, with only the disciples near him, he asked them, 'Who do the crowds say that I am?'" (Mark 6:46 and Luke 9:18). At others times contemplative prayer helped him discern the direction of his life: the temptations in the wilderness, the experiences on Mount Tabor, and the struggles in the garden of Gethsemane.

Listening as Withdrawal

The same pattern of withdrawal was the hallmark of the desert fathers and mothers. When a person desired a life of solitude, they would seek an elder and say, "Give me a word." The response was, "Go to your cell and your cell will teach you everything." The cell was the physical venue for the process of transformation that would take place within the monk. Eventually, *the monk would become what he or she experienced in the cell*. It began and was sustained with various forms of listening as Jesus had exhorted his disciples: go into your inner room. This intentional form of listening requires a place of solitude and as much silence as possible.

Listening, regardless of what one's "desert" is, forms a fundamental aspect of transformation: *withdrawal*. Transformation is often initiated by awareness that the surface of life is incomplete. Like Arsenius, we desire something more real and complete. This opens a path of spiritual formation that includes prayer, openness to self-knowledge, humble dependence on God, and love of neighbor. There is a definite sense of "leaving" or withdrawing from the dominance of conventional life, even for short periods, in order to find a venue for the slow process of transformation. The primary purpose is to "gain perspective on the world and its values." [14]

Contemplative prayer is an integral venue for withdrawal. Its various disciplines (such as centering prayer, imageless contemplation, *lectio divina*, walking meditation, etc.) take us away from and "silence" our customary daily patterns of thinking and activities so that we can "read the water." Raimon Panikkar identifies three important areas of withdrawal: the silence of intellect, the silence of the will, and the silence of action.[15] By "dying" to our thoughts, desires, and actions, we can see them and ourselves in a new light through a change of consciousness: "Withdrawal, then, does not mean flight and evasion but making the hard and difficult journey closer to one's true self, which is where God is."[16] As we shall see, this withdrawal must be balanced by (and indeed makes possible) compassionate relationships with other people and compassionate stewardship of the Earth. Tim Vivian points out that the centripetal movement of withdrawal and the centrifugal energy of love form the dynamic reality of transformation.[17]

Two: Experiencing and Being Formed by God's Presence

Guard the good treasure entrusted to you,
with the help of the Holy Spirit living in us.
—2 TIM. 1:4

Abba Arsenius learned from his desert mentor, Abba John the Dwarf, that he must commit himself to an inner life of various forms of contemplative prayer. This praxis of prayer gradually shaped and formed God's presence in him. His cell and the praxis within it became his venue for abiding in God and overcoming the self-centered focus of his life. Arsenius discovered that the arena for his transformation was the presence of God within him and in his mentors, like John. Arsenius's path toward transformation took him away from the city. His path is not the path for everyone, yet what he learned in embracing a major change in his life is filled with wisdom for all. Through his willingness to embrace the change in his life, he experienced *a healing of the soul* that made space for being formed into the "full stature of Christ" (Eph. 4:13).

Arsenius's new life reached beyond a mere change of occupation or venue. He let go of one system of fundamental values to embrace another. His spiritual transformation was not to another way of experiencing life but to another mode of existence. His new life was not a rejection of life in the world or a renunciation of his bodily existence. It was a transformation from a false self of his own creation to a true self. Some people might want to tell Arsenius to "get real," but that is precisely what happened! Although contemplative prayer was an integral part of his new life, it was not its goal. Contemplative experience was a channel for living water that nourished the seeds that formed and sustained the life that flowed from communion of his soul with the fullness and will of God.

Contemplative "Reality Check"

In November 2005 I spent five days with the Coptic monks of St. Macarius Monastery in Wadi El-Natrun (Scetis), Egypt. The monastery was founded by Marcarius the Great in CE 367 and was the home of John the Dwarf. I was invited to enter into the rhythm of their day that included vigils and chanting of psalms in the early morning hours from three to six. Later each day I walked in the desert surrounding the monastery and sat in the ruins where elders like John the Dwarf and Arsenius had lived. I held pottery shards from pots, cups, and plates the ancient monks had used. I could sense their presence and the power of their ascetic lives. I realized that the contemplative praxis of the ancient and modern monks is, indeed, a discipline that "guards the treasure entrusted" to them and myself. Contemplative prayer is not just a venue for a change of consciousness; it is a form of stewardship that *cares for the transformed life that God makes possible in us.*[18] Although the monks of St. Macarius live a way of life that is physically and socially isolated, their life of prayer, daily rhythm of work, and commitment to God's presence in the Bible provide contemplative awareness of a dimension of life that is *everywhere.* When I asked Brother Jerome to "give me a word," he said, "You do not have to come here to find Jesus; he lives where you live!"

Three: Manifesting the Presence
of God in Our Lives

As we have seen, human transformation begins in prayer. Prayer, in its variety of forms, is a simple abiding in God. It is a mutual seeing. We learn to see as God sees, and the energies of God become our energies.

Rather than separating us from the world, prayer engages us more fully with the world. As we experience God's love, we become "partakers of the divine nature" and *collaborate with God in the ongoing creation of the world*. God's energies become incarnate as compassion that responds to the suffering, pain, and inequities present in modern life. Compassion is not a commodity to be shared or legislated by the strong for the weak. It is the intimacy and life-giving energy that flows from the elimination of the unnecessary boundaries and barriers we erect for survival, control, and protection. Compassion is the grace to go beyond ourselves and find communion with others. *We learn this from our contemplative experience of God's presence in our lives.* The Word becomes flesh and dwells among us again!

Arsenius, John the Dwarf, and the modern monks of St. Macarius remind me that their withdrawal to monastic life and my withdrawal to contemplative prayer are authentic when they give birth to the fruits of the Spirit in our daily lives. The stewardship of our life of prayer will lead to compassionate living. The enclosed life of the monks of Wadi El-Natrun models a dependence on God that breaks down the self-imposed and limiting boundaries of human self-reliance. They remind us that in the midst of our technology, frenzy for effectiveness and progress, and our genuine desire to resolve conflicts and solve the challenges of today's world, we must not depend on ourselves. When possibilities are limited to our own vision and resources, we create a lifeless desert of ever-increasing activity. Unless we take time, with patience, to withdraw to a daily rhythm of awareness of God's presence, we will get lost in the self-importance of what we do and miss seeing the sacred dimension of our work and the people around us. We will lose our center and scatter our spirits. Our self-reliance will stifle the effectiveness of what we can accomplish and limit the horizon of what is possible.

In the desert of Egypt the burden of my awareness of the needs of the world and the personal weight that I feel on my narrow shoulders were given new hope. The horizons of my own life were extended. The monks of Macarius have not left the world! The whole world is present in their lives. Their patient attention to God's presence enables them *to live in that presence.* They inspire my own practice of contemplative prayer and remind me that the future of human society and the fecundity of our relationship

with the Earth depend on our willingness to slow
down and find a rhythm of listening with our ears
and our hearts. Our contemplative openness to God
is the womb of our love for our neighbor and the
Earth.

CONCLUSION

Contemplation and action are complementary
dimensions of God's presence in the world. Like the
great icons of the Eastern Christian churches, our
ordinary lives and actions can become windows that
draw others into an experience of God's presence
and redeeming power. Our daily work and relationships, passions and joys, sins and repentance, search
for knowledge and creative expression, and engagement with the challenges and opportunities of life
are venues for God's presence in the world.

The communion with God that we experience
in contemplative prayer is an *eternal relationship*
because God is eternal. The resurrection of Jesus
lies at the center of Christian belief and living. The
union with God that Jesus experienced transcended
human mortality. This central mystery of Christian
life declares that, when God is present in human life,
human death becomes a threshold linking our finite
life to the transcendent and eternal life of God. Even
in death, human life continues to be transformed.
This pattern of life, death, and transformation is

embedded in all creation. It is the Paschal Mystery in which we are drawn into the reality of death and eternal life each day of our lives. The contemplative dimension of the Gospel proclaims that we live simultaneously in the contexts of who we are now and who we shall be in our completion in God. We, and all creation, exist in this present finite cosmos and at the same time in an eternal fullness, which will ultimately be realized in God. Jesus taught that it is in giving ourselves to God's image in us that we find this fullness of life. By dying to self-made worlds and limited vision, we find ourselves transformed and made whole through the vision and tangible presence of God. This is the consciousness to which we are called. Contemplative prayer is our faithful mentor along this path.

Chapter 6

Binding Head and Heart:
*A Conversation Concerning
Theological Education:
The Contemplative Ministry Project*

David G. R. Keller

> *In all our thoughts and actions we ought to
> remember the presence of God.*
> —Bernard of Clairvaux

In the summer of 2002 the Fund for Theological Education convened its annual conference for theological students at the school of theology and seminary at St. John's University in Collegeville, Minnesota. An opportunity for contemplative prayer and a discussion of personal prayer in the lives of clergy was the most heavily attended of the many workshops offered at the conference. Emily Wilmer and I led the workshop in the oratory at the Episcopal House of Prayer on the campus of St. John's University. Students expressed two concerns, both evidently deeply felt. First, they wanted more room for contemplative prayer, spiritual formation, and the study of the rich traditions of Christian spirituality in their graduate theological education. They acknowledged that the curriculum was already overloaded and too stressful, and yet they expressed the need for mentoring in personal prayer to be their highest priority. Their second concern was how they would be able to integrate a pattern of personal prayer into the busy ministries demanded of them after graduation and ordination. Newly ordained men and women at the workshop affirmed these concerns from their own experiences. I have heard similar concerns from clergy, seminary deans and faculty, and laity throughout the church. The workshop in Collegeville was not an isolated event. Voices throughout the church express the same concerns.

A Challenge for the Church and Its Formation of Lay and Ordained Leaders

What were the theological students at Collegeville asking from theological education? Their voices are linked with many others in their call for a balance between cognitive learning and spiritual formation. They are telling the church and its theological educators that they want to be more than masters of knowledge and skills for ministry. Embedded in their questions and frustrations is a vision of the persons that they want to be as church leaders. The concerns of these students, and of clergy and lay professionals already in active ministries throughout the church, reflect more than frustration with heavy work expectations. They are telling the church how much it is neglecting prayer in the formation of its leaders and communicants. They are saying that theological education—with its emphasis on academic work and "practical" fieldwork—is not relating to the whole person. They are frustrated with the current way that readiness for ministry is defined by that kind of theological education. They are asking for more attention to the relationship between the formation of Christian leaders and the God in whom we believe.

The concerns expressed in Collegeville raise some fundamental questions about theological education and life in the church today. Who defines the shape of ministries in today's church? How should our lay and ordained leaders be educated, formed, and prepared for ministries? Why has our epistemology devalued spiritual formation and contemplative prayer as valid and necessary forms of knowledge? By whose authority is "readiness for ministry" determined? What does this passionate recognition of the fundamental need for personal prayer in theological education tell us about the life of the church?

Some schools of theology and seminaries are already addressing these issues with programs in spiritual formation, centers of spirituality, and courses

on applied spirituality. This chapter is one response
to this critical need and describes a project dedicated
to facilitating conversations about the role of spiritual formation in theological education and the formation of a network to facilitate further sharing of
experience, resources, and opportunities. All agree
that more people should join the conversations.

CONTEMPLATION AND ACTION IN MINISTRY:
A SCATTERED GIFT

The Episcopal Church's "Outline of the Faith"
clearly states a truth common to all denominations: the ministry of the church is shared by laypersons and clergy. The outline also states that all
Christians are to work, pray, and give for the spread
of the kingdom of God. This challenge is repeated
in the fourth form of the "Prayers of the People"
in the Holy Eucharist where the congregation asks
God to "guide the people of this land, and of all
the nations, in the ways of justice and peace; that
we may honor one another and serve the common
good." [1] This is a tall order, and the outline makes
it clear that none of us can fulfill our ministries
without the grace of God and intentional corporate
and personal prayer.

Human beings and the grace of God are the gifts
that make it possible to "honor one another and
serve the common good." Prayer is the mystery that

bonds these sacred gifts together. Yet when we look honestly at ourselves, the activities of the church, the overworked lives of clergy, the often frenetic manner in which the church trains lay and ordained leaders, and the society of the twenty-first century, we find a great deal more reliance on human activity than on prayer. This does not imply that the ministries of countless laypersons and clergy are not filled with compassion, hard work, and sacrifice. The church continues to be faithful in its witness for justice and peace and its ministries to human need. At the same time it is hard to deny our frustrations in the midst of world conflicts, serious health and hunger crises, institutional greed, religious intolerance, and growing national hegemonies that create and feed fear and lack of respect among human beings. It is hard to deny the pressures and expectations of a postmodern society that seems to need constant drivenness and ever-growing materialism. Cell phones, pagers, and multitasking have become the icons of our modern drive for "survival" and the stresses that it creates in our lives. The church and its leaders are just as busy as everyone else. Our lives are becoming increasingly scattered, and we are losing touch with our divine center. We are so noisy that we are losing the art of listening to each other and to God. We are so busy that we are losing sight of what it means to be human. This situation is truly diabolic. What are we becoming in our hyperactivity? Churches are just as busy as society at large. Are we being good stewards of our sacred human lives and the grace of God?

Awareness of God who is in and around us is the source of compassion, responsible living, and justice. We must integrate our desire for progress and solutions with a receptivity and response to the wisdom of God. The dysfunctions, injustices, and stresses of modern society are all related to a lack of vision that drives us to be satisfied with superficiality. We have developed an insatiable appetite to live on the surface of life. As we become more and more starved for what is fundamental and meaningful, we join the frenzy of activity and desire for material satisfaction that may dance around but never lead us to the center of our being. We are becoming pathologically scattered.

Human history and the wisdom of the world's religions proclaim that the stresses of the modern age—its conflicts, pain, and injustices—will not be overcome by the design of new institutions, the application of greater financial resources to more innovative programs, military or economic coercion, technology, or super-human effort. What is needed is a change in human consciousness, a transformation in the way that we see each other and the world.

This transformed vision, the bonding of human beings with the grace of God, is the heart of personal prayer and contemplation. Contemplative prayer is crucial to the challenges of our era. It is an emptying of self to gain one's self. It is a letting-go of control to become a vessel of reconciliation and transformation. In its rejection of self-interest, it is totally countercultural, and yet at the same time it is perhaps the single most practical needed thing in the postmodern world. It is also one of the fundamental dimensions of the Christian gospel and way of life. How can the church encourage, form, and support personal contemplative prayer in the lives of the laity and its lay and ordained leaders?

THEOLOGICAL EDUCATION:
AN INTEGRATION OF LEARNING AND PRAYER

Theological education should not define ministry. It exists to enable and support a variety of ministries and root them in the experience of God and the vision and wisdom of our many faith traditions. The goal of theological education is not mastery of theology, prayer, biblical study, church history, liturgy, moral theology, pastoral care, or church leadership. It is providing opportunities and disciplines for personal transformation through experience of God, self-awareness, and participation in a learning community that will root a person's ministry and continuing spiritual formation in the richness of the Christian way of life. Theological education is a fundamental resource for ministry, but ministry itself proceeds from intimacy with God.[2] This intimacy is conceived by God, born in a pattern of personal prayer, formed through participation in a faith-community, and made tangible through a personal engagement with the life of the world.

A school of theology or seminary should, above all, be an environment of grace wherein Christ becomes tangible in the lives of faculty, staff, and students and in its disciplines of learning, worship, and community life. A student's experience of God in personal prayer will enable her or him to recognize God's presence within theology, scripture, church history, liturgy, pastoral care, and the skills of church leadership. This integration of head and heart, of *theologia mentis* and *theologia cordis*, is essential if we are to form lay and ordained Christian leaders as whole persons. One of the foundations of the patristic period was "a loving search for God, not only an intellectual search, but also a spiritual search, an advance in holiness." [3] This emphasis comes directly from the teaching of Jesus, who recognized the heart, the inner chamber of intimacy with God, as the source of our words and actions. The wisdom of the desert fathers and mothers and of Benedictine spirituality emphasizes the critical role of contemplative listening in a person's path toward self-awareness, wisdom, and transformation. In like manner, today's students of theology and religion, in listening to God in daily contemplative prayer and meditation on scripture, will be enabled to hear that same voice in their academic work, research and writing, corporate worship, fieldwork, and the common life of the learning community.

If this is true, we must be open to considering changes in some practical aspects of theological education. (I am grateful to Tilden Edwards for raising the following issues.) In what ways will an integration of cognitive learning and spiritual formation change the methods of classroom instruction? How can cognitive learning and training in pastoral skills be integrated with ascetic disciplines essential for personal transformation? How can a student's experiences of God's love, wisdom, and guidance in prayer be integrated with their study of scripture, theology, history, liturgy, and so on?

Another consequence of an integration of personal prayer and the academic disciplines of theological education is that each student will learn to discover God's faithful presence in the varied life of the learning community and to contribute her or his unique and growing experience of God and personal learning and struggles to the community. In this way, theological education becomes a dynamic experience of transformation for both the student and the learning community. The stability of the learning community provides an external grace-filled venue for the development of an internal stability of heart in each student. The result is not mastery of intellectual or ascetic disciplines but

an experience of the mystery of God's transforming grace. This, too, reflects the experience of the
Christian desert elders who learned that in addition
to conventional knowledge and external behavior a
person must come to know her or his "inner ground"
and the movement of God's spirit within. This contemplative knowledge of one's self and God extends
the boundaries of a person's awareness of God and
self. It is a letting-go of conventional knowledge and
self-image to collaborate with the mind of Christ,
and it enables one's vision and experience of life to
be more complete. It makes the *eschaton* of God's
desires for creation present in the formation and
hard work of each student.

The formation of a life of prayer during theological education will not only form and support
students during their formal education, but it will
also ground each student in a spiritual path pattern of prayer that will support their ministries
after graduation. Students will become mentors in
personal prayer and the wisdom and resources of
our rich Christian traditions of spirituality. This
does not mean that they will graduate with a static
praxis and list of resources. They will know from
experience that growth of the soul and mind is an
endless journey into the mystery of God, who will
illumine and guide their intellectual and spiritual
growth and empower their loving action for the
rest of their lives.

The fundamental mission of theological education is both to provide opportunities for persons to
become rooted and grounded in God and to guide,
form, and empower them with the knowledge and
skills for understanding and applying scripture,
theology, history, worship, and traditions of our
Christian faith communities in the contexts of a variety of ministries. This mission requires attention to
academic, pastoral, and leadership disciplines—and
formation in the disciplines of personal prayer.

The evaluation of students' progress must not be
limited to traditional methods that measure cognitive learning and practical skills for ministry. How
can educators discern personal transformation and
inner spiritual development? How can faculty, spiritual directors, and fieldwork supervisors discern and
guide the growing maturity of the whole person?
How can accrediting institutions and judicatory
authorities become involved in discussions about
these questions and eventually ask for assessment of
spiritual formation along with competency in cognitive learning and ministerial skills?

ON BEING FAITHFUL TO THE ROOTS
AND WISDOM OF OUR TRADITION

*Tradition is not the preservation of certain
relics of the past, but is the presence with
us now of powers of life and understanding
without whom we should indeed be orphans.* [4]

Our schools of theology and seminaries excel in providing access to the roots and continued fullness of our various Christian faith traditions. These essential academic disciplines rely on intellectual data and skills as the primary way of knowing. They rely on research techniques to gather information and on writing skills and dialogue to articulate and synthesize learning. They rely, also, on practical experience in homiletics, pastoral care, church administration, liturgy, and leadership skills. These disciplines provide indispensable knowledge and learning tools for the ministries and life-long learning of church leaders.

ON BEING FAITHFUL TO
EXPERIENCE OF GOD IN PRAYER

The man or woman whose life is colored by prayer, whose loving communion with God comes first, will always wins souls; because he or she shows in their own life and person the attractiveness of reality, the demand, the transforming power of the spiritual life. His or her intellectual powers and the rest will not, comparatively speaking, matter much. The point is that such a man or woman stands as a witness to that which he or she proclaims. [5]

Schools of theology and seminaries are entrusted, also, to form their students in the disciplines of personal prayer. Theological education must equip our lay and ordained leaders for life in the twenty-first century by helping these women and men integrate the rich traditions of Christian spirituality with twenty-first-century life. This requires that students be introduced to and learn to practice a variety of forms of personal contemplative prayer and spiritual practices. They should be given opportunities to develop a disciplined pattern of prayerful living that fills and integrates their work, relationships, continuing learning and growth, service and recreation with the experience and vitality of God. Since there are many forms of contemplative prayer and the personalities and needs of students are diverse, a practicum could include introductions to imageless contemplative prayer, guided meditation, centering prayer, *lectio divina*, journaling, use of sabbath time, retreats, creative expression, care of body and mind, discernment, spiritual direction, and reflection on the relationships between prayer and study, work, ministry, and societal issues. Eventually, each student should be encouraged to settle into a form of silent contemplative prayer that will enable her or him to experience God's presence in a personal way each day. Other practices may also help integrate personal prayer with academic learning and fieldwork. This foundation of personal prayer should complement the corporate worship of the learning community and will remain with the student after he or she graduates. Individual members of the faculty and staff could be assigned to students as mentors and help them form a personal pattern of prayer. This would enable students to experience faculty and staff as persons whose personal faith motivates and empowers their vocations as teachers and staff.

In addition to a personal praxis of prayer, schools of theology and seminaries should require courses that will introduce students to the history of Christian spirituality, its various movements within history, its influence on society, and the lives and writings of influential Christian spiritual leaders and ascetics. Ideally, this course of study should be integrated in an inter-disciplinary manner with other courses such as scripture, church history, and theology. These courses should include attention to the richness and integrity of other world religious traditions and their influence on Christianity and society.

A More Inclusive Epistemology

A more complete spiritual formation of theological students relies on an epistemology that integrates cognitive knowledge and experiences within the affective domain. It seeks experience of God as well as knowledge about God. It seeks spiritual empowerment of ministry as well as ministerial skills. It forms the person who will benefit from and implement the academic learning.

Spiritual formation and personal prayer are often optional components of graduate theological education. They are usually held in lower esteem than the academic disciplines because the epistemology of graduate institutions prefers intellectual inquiry and cognitive reflection as the primary ways of knowing. Although academic knowledge and proficiency in pastoral and leadership skills are more easily evaluated than "prayerful living," the inner life of a theological student is also of great value to God: "Your inner self, the unfading beauty of a gentle and quiet spirit is of great worth in God's sight" (1 Peter 3:4). John Main, OSB, one of the most respected contemplative mentors of the twentieth century, puts it more bluntly: "The call to meditate is an invitation to stop leading our lives on the basis of second-hand evidence." [6] Cognitive knowledge, which values primary sources, is different from but no more important than formation in a life of prayer, which values experience of the One who is the source of life. They are both essential ways of knowing and, when valued as complementary, provide a more nearly complete vision of life and empowerment for ministry. The early church valued intellectual learning and contemplative prayer as equally valid forms of knowledge. [7] Evelyn Underhill, one of the most influential twentieth-century Anglican spiritual writers, encouraged clergy to seek the Word of God daily in the deep foundation of silence that lies within each person. And she reminded clergy and laity alike that our vocation is to listen to that Word and to live according to what we hear.[8] Schools of theology and seminaries must develop this continuum in the lives of students: the vocation to lay and ordained ministries and the vocation to listen to the Word. How else will the Word become tangible in the lives and ministries of our church leaders?

The "reign" of cognitive learning in the epistemology of schools of theology and seminaries and a pervading suspicion of "applied spirituality" are facts of life in modern theological education. And we cannot deny that sometimes the predominance of pressures to succeed in academic studies inhibit a student's faith development and longing for a more personal awareness of God's presence in their theological education and personal lives. These issues must be mentioned in this chapter primarily to encourage further discussion. At the same time, the fruits of spiritual formation in graduate theological education must be clearly articulated, even though they will require unique methods of evaluation in the context of granting degrees.

Here are a few more questions for discussion. What do students and graduates of schools of theology and seminaries desire for the people among whom they will live and serve? Does their graduate theological education enable them to become what they desire for others? Does "readiness for ministry" include manifesting the intimacy, wisdom, and compassion of God as well as competency in pastoral care, biblical and theological literacy, parish administration, and so on? How does being a person of prayer enable and ennoble these traditional competencies? How does theological education root people in God so that they, in turn, may till the ground for others who yearn to be rooted in God?

THE ORIGINS OF THE
MINISTRIES OF THE CHURCH

It is worth repeating that the work of theological education is not to define the church's ministries. It is equally important to acknowledge that the church is not the creation of human beings—in particular, it is not created by church leaders. The Bible is clear that every local faith community and denomination is a diverse community of persons who have been gathered by the inner and dynamic activity of God's spirit. We do not create or sustain the church or the "kingdom of God." We are invited to enter a community whose purpose is to make the realm of God tangible in society and to collaborate with God's grace to form an environment whose sole purpose is to manifest God's presence and love in its common life. The simple purpose of the church is to acknowledge that all persons are created in the image of God and to form its members so that they may embody the likeness of God in their values and manner of life. This is the source of the vital link between head and heart, prayer and action, and church and community.

Therefore, it is the church, guided by the Spirit who has gathered it, that discerns its ministries. There are at least five elements that help the church in its communal life to discern its ministries and therefore the direction of theological education:

- An awareness that, in the words of Peter, we are called to "become participants of the divine nature" (2 Peter 1:4) and to manifest the Trinitarian life of God in the world.

- The life of God, present in the community of believers through the dynamic and creative energies of the Holy Spirit.

- A vision of authentic human life present in the Bible and, for the Christian community, in the life of Jesus of Nazareth.

- A biblical vision of the unity and goodness of all creation—the sacredness of life—that becomes the source of the church's compassionate response to the life of the world, manifested by care for the environment, honoring one another, and serving the common good.

- The challenges and needs of the world in each generation.

THE CHURCH AS A
CONTEMPLATIVE COMMUNITY

Prayer is the source of the church's life and ministries. Prayer is the stream of love that constitutes the
life of God and is therefore the model for the life
of the church. A person learns to pray by placing
himself or herself in the flow of the energy of God.
The mutual flow of that energy between each person and God is the heart of contemplative prayer. It
is "knowledge" of God in the biblical sense of intimate experience. Contemplative prayer is nothing
less than participating in the divine nature (2 Peter
1:3–4). It evokes a radical change of consciousness in
the way we see the world and what we desire for the
world (2 Peter 1:5–11). The plenitude of each person's compassionate relationship with the world lies
in that person's prayerful experience of God's love.
Compassion becomes an intense desire rather than
a duty or the fulfillment of a commandment. The
responses of the early church to the life of Jesus demonstrate that the heart of Christian life and ministry
is the development of purity of heart, humility, and
charity. These virtues take time to be formed in us
and require immense self-giving: "Prayer, which is
the fruit of true conversion, is an activity, an adventure, and sometimes a dangerous one, since there are
occasions when it brings neither peace nor comfort,
but challenge, conflict, and new responsibility." [9]

The church is called to be a contemplative community because it lives within and is committed to the world and at the same time is called to discern the mystery of God's presence in and desires for the world. Practicing this contemplative vocation makes discerning God's voice possible and is the womb of the church's corporate and social ministries. How can the church be a contemplative community unless its leaders are formed in a contemplative life of prayer and equipped—from first-hand experience—to mentor the faith communities that they serve in the same life of prayer?

Any soul that penetrates within, just by doing so, deepens the church and the church's consciousness of herself. It thus calls the church, as though from depth to depth, in the realization of her own mystery. Each Christian, each group of the faithful, in effect, expresses and manifests in itself the *Una Catholica* as a whole, and in her, the only Lord. That is precisely the irreplaceable role, the very service of contemplatives in the church. [10]

THE CONTEMPLATIVE MINISTRY PROJECT

In June of 2002 Father Thomas Keating and I began a process of contacting twelve mentors in contemplative prayer whose lives and teaching have influenced theological education and whose ministries have encouraged the relationship between contemplative prayer and an active engagement in society. Our efforts were funded by the Trust for the Meditation Process in Minneapolis, Minnesota. Two of the trust's staff, Carole Baker and Martha Bolinger, assisted with planning, along with Diane Fassel. We convened a group of twelve persons at St. Benedict's Abbey in Snowmass, Colorado, in October 2003. [11] Over four days we set out to discern—through contemplative prayer, group discussion, and writing groups—responses to the following questions: What is the contemplative dimension of the Gospel? How have you experienced it in your life and ministry? What is its place within Christian faith and life? What is the rationale for including contemplative practice and the study of Christian spirituality in the curricula of schools of theology and seminaries? How can we facilitate ongoing conversation with those who have a stake in theological education?

The sharing and discussion were deeply personal and related to the church's life and to the serious challenges and issues facing us all. We looked for key ideas and common threads. It became clear that, with several denominations present, we must learn each other's theological language and seek statements that we could all accept. Our first challenge was to discover what we meant by "contemplative prayer." [12] The statement that emerged is as follows:

A Description of Contemplative Prayer

In response to Jesus' call for personal transformation, contemplative prayer is a grace-filled attentiveness to God that initiates and sustains a change of consciousness leading to love of God and neighbor.

This understanding of contemplative prayer comes from awareness that Christian contemplation:

- is grounded in Holy Scripture;
- is grounded in experience of the Christian community;
- embraces a variety of practices that sustain our ability, as St. Paul exhorts, to "pray always";
- is a constant presence throughout Holy Scripture: Exod. 14:14, Ps. 62:1–2, Ps. 141:1–2, Mark 1:35, Mark 13:32–37, Matt. 6:5–6, John 15:1–5, and Thess. 4:17, etc.).

After almost two days of sharing and meditation, our second challenge was to form a statement of our understanding of "the contemplative dimension of the Gospel." Here is our summary:

*Summary Statement Developed
and Accepted by Participants*

The Gospel is the core of Christian living. It has within it a contemplative dimension. This dimension is God's invitation to every human being, through Jesus Christ, to share

God's very nature. It begins as a way of listening with ears, eyes, and heart. It grows as a desire to know God and to enter into God's love. This is made possible through a dying to self or emptying of self that becomes a radical listening to God and experience of God's love. Through a pattern of abiding in God that we call contemplative prayer, a change of consciousness takes place. This dynamic sharing of God's nature forms each person and opens them to the mind and very life of Christ, challenging them to be instruments of God's love and energy in the world. This contemplative consciousness bonds each person in a union with God and all other persons. It enables them to find God present in all things. This transformed and self-giving love is nurtured and guided in Christian faith communities through Holy Scripture, sacraments, and faithful spiritual prayer practices.

The latter part of our time together was used to discern the implications of the contemplative dimension of the Gospel for theological education. Here is our statement:

> *What is the Rationale for Including the Contemplative Dimension of the Gospel and Contemplative Prayer in the Curricula of Seminaries and Schools of Theology?*

Contemplative prayer is a fundamental dimension of the Gospel of Jesus Christ. Therefore it

should be an essential component in the preparation of leaders in the Church.

The capacity for contemplative prayer and
awareness is inborn in humans.

Every person has a calling to contemplative
prayer and is incomplete without this.

Because acquiring the Mind of Christ is essential to Christian living, it is essential that spiritual leaders acquire this identity with Christ.
This call to acquire an identity with the mind
of Christ assumes that:

- A transformation of consciousness is part
  of the Christian life.
- Contemplative prayer is necessary for the
  integration of theological teachings.
- Contemplative prayer invites and sustains
  a change of consciousness.

Because the Gospel invites all to communion
with Christ, it is essential that all spiritual
leaders be mentored in and taught ways to
enter more deeply into intimacy with Christ.

Because contemplative prayer results in fruits
called for in the Gospels that are essential to
Christianity, every Christian leader should be
given the opportunity to learn this prayer in
its many forms.

The training of the Church's lay and ordained
leaders in contemplative prayer is essential if

the Church is to remain faithful to the mission entrusted to it by Christ:

- Jesus' teaching and his own life of prayer demonstrate that the kingdom of God becomes known and effective in our lives through contemplation.
- Contemplative prayer opens a person's heart and mind to address problems of violence, racism, poverty, and other forms of systemic evil that threaten our world.
- Attentiveness to God in contemplation affects the whole person and will support Christian leaders in many aspects of their lives and ministries. The source of this spiritual nurture and health is rooted in experience of the love of God in prayer and manifested in the exercise of the gifts and fruits of the Spirit in ministry. Contemplative prayer is an experience of the Paschal Mystery that links the leaders' work to the self-giving of God.

GOALS AND PROGRAM OF THE CONTEMPLATIVE MINISTRY PROJECT

After the gathering at Snowmass in October 2003, the project has continued its work through a steering committee and has approved the following projects:

- Development of a list of persons and institutions who are interested in participating in the Project's conversations and goals.

- Planning and facilitating four regional meetings each year for the next three years to continue conversations, share resources and ideas, and plan projects that will help integrate spiritual formation, contemplative prayer, and the study of Christian spirituality into the curricula of schools of theology and seminaries.

- Development of a prototype and initial pilot versions of "An Experience in Contemplative Ministry," a one- to three-week experience in contemplative life and ministry for theological students and current church leaders (similar to the Clinical Pastoral Education model, but with a different purpose).

- Development of a network promoting the Contemplative Ministry Project's goals and linking the project's participants and goals as well as other programs and resources with similar goals.

- Solicitation of financial support for the project through grants and other sources. [13]

Chapter 7

Centering Prayer and the Work of Clergy and Congregations:
Prayer, Priests, and the Postmodern World

Paul David Lawson

The Ministry

THIS CHAPTER EXAMINES the work of clergy in the modern congregation. The twenty-first century is a time of extreme societal anxiety, and this anxiety can be transmitted through social groups, including congregations. High levels of anxious energy can have an impact on the ability of the ministers and congregation to function in a healthy manner. Clergy often become targets for anxiety, which can lead them to stress and burnout. Through the practice of centering prayer, however, they can effectively monitor and control their reactions to the energy of anxiety. By doing this for themselves, they can thereby act as immune systems for their congregations, transforming the negative energy of anxiety into creative energy available to empower new ministry and growth.

Soon after I was ordained, I remember a friend of mine from seminary telling me that his daughter, Aiden, had been asked, as part of a group exercise in kindergarten, to tell the class what her father did at work. She thought for a few minutes and then replied, "He drinks wine and reads books and talks a lot." Twenty-five years ago that was a good description by a five-year-old of the work of a priest—and probably a more accurate and knowledgeable description than most adults could offer. The work of the clergy was shrouded in mystery, symbolized in some orthodox denominations by the celebration of the Eucharist taking place behind a screen, or fictionalized in books such as G. K. Chesterton's thrillers or movies such as "Going My Way."

Either way, the popular belief was that the work of the priest occurred on Sundays at the altar and in the pulpit, where the minister read from a book, drank wine, and talked. In some denominations the minister shared the wine with the congregation, and in other denominations he merely read and talked. Most members of the congregation could have agreed with Aiden's description with slight modifications for their own interests, such as home visitation, Episcopal Church Women meetings, or invocations at city council meetings. The role of a minister in the 1970s was reasonably well defined, at least in the popular imagination; almost everyone, including clergy, knew what ministers were supposed to be doing.

Seminary training concentrated on Bible studies, preaching, theology, and the traditional subjects that prepared a person to go into the parish and do the daily work of visiting members of the congregation, calling on people in the hospital, preparing a sermon each week, overseeing the maintenance of the church facilities, and meeting with various guilds and committees. The priest often had time to engage in various social and community ministries or activities. Many times, ministers would give one day a week to jail visitation or to work in a home for seniors or an orphanage. This predictable availability enabled some dioceses, like Los Angeles, to build institutions based on the clergy giving one or two days a week of their time.

In our own patch of Christendom in the Anglican Communion, some clergy and congregations did their work with incense and gongs, others with sermons and songs, but we all knew what we were supposed to be doing and why we trained for it. Then we went out and did it.

Toward the end of the 1970s, it became more difficult to understand the role of the clergy. As more women entered the workplace, there were fewer people to visit during the day. As workday commutes lengthened, fewer people were available to work on church projects at night. There were fewer church meetings. Because of the increased emphasis on separation of church and state, fewer city councils were interested in invocations. I was asked recently to do an invocation on the condition that I omit any reference to God for fear that somebody in the community might be offended. "Invoking what?" I asked.

In terms of society at large, the social upheavals of the 1960s and 1970s (which included changing cultural values, music, life styles, gender roles, and what it meant to be a family) all contributed to uncertainty among clergy. Edwin Friedman in his book *Failure of Nerve: Leadership in the Age of the Quick Fix* argues that from the 1960s onward society as a whole became increasingly anxious. This anxiety was amplified by the media and fed back to the institutions of society, which in turn became more anxious.[1] This anxiety led to a decrease in functioning and the inability to make decisions or take personal responsibility for one's own actions. This in turn led to a crisis in leadership whereby issues were never resolved but transformed into another entity. Consequently, institutions such as churches became more reactive to the smallest issues, encouraging everyone to do the same thing or believe the same way or be ostracized. Scapegoats were found to explain problems, and any quick fix was better than a permanent solution that involved long-term pain. Trying to lead congregations in this milieu of confusion became impossible.

The loss of homogeneity within both society and church led to confusion among clergy as to what they were supposed to be doing. For example, Sunday school material in the early 1970s reflected an intact nuclear family while at the same time the students in the Sunday schools were often products of newly broken homes. Seminaries were teaching classes in counseling divorced couples while some dioceses were excluding these same couples from the church altogether. What were clergy to do? Were they supposed to be teaching or preaching, reconciling or admonishing, upholding the very framework of society or leading the revolution? There was no consensus among denominations or among clergy themselves. This in turn led to a further increase of anxiety in virtually everyone.

Anxiety comes in two types: acute and chronic. Acute anxiety is worry and concern about a specific problem or situation such as a car that will not start. The solution is evident. Take the car to a mechanic. The car is fixed, and the anxiety is relieved. Chronic anxiety is, however, the more common form, and is characterized by worry and concern about things that have not happened and yet may happen in the future. That kind of issue cannot be resolved, and so anxiety builds in institutions and persons, often leading to a release of tension by way of violence.

As a result of the changing conditions in society, clergy began to suffer identity crises. As we have said, they were unsure of themselves and unsure about what they were supposed to be doing. This was not the first time that clergy had felt a need to reinvent themselves as society changed around them. Throughout the history of the church, its clergy have had to redefine their roles in relation to society. One such period was at the close of the nineteenth century. Barbara Ehrenreich in her book *Fear of Falling* suggests that the professionalization of the middle class took place between 1870 and 1920. [2] It is Ehrenreich's contention that the middle class was created to be a broker between the upper and lower classes. Before that period anyone could be a broker or a manager, and in many cases you were what you said you were. Barbers were dentists and dentists were doctors. Jobs that were considered professions were very loosely regulated. But now doctors, lawyers, and clergy from the mainline denominations were among groups that chose to "professionalize." What professionalization meant was that a university education was required as an entry level for practice. This requirement did two things. It restricted entry to the profession, thereby creating a job market, and it carved out a niche located someplace between the lower and upper classes. Lawyers, doctors, and ministers all declared themselves professional, scientific, and modern, a group set apart from both the poor working class and the idle rich. Tradition, intuition, and guesswork were replaced with science and rationality. A degree replaced the old reading for orders in ministry and for the practice of law. At a time when only five percent of the country went to college, this provision guaranteed that only gentlemen would qualify for these newly minted professions. With each succeeding generation, the need for more specialized training increased. In the United States the basic clergy degree was inflated from a Bachelor of Divinity to a Master of Divinity. In the present millennium a Doctorate of Ministry is considered the *basic* degree for rectors of larger congregations, and for those clergy seeking advancement to the episcopate.

One would think that, with these degrees, clergy would have some sense of what it was they were to do in their work and ministry. Alas, that is not the case. Even with all of these degrees, what clergy study, unlike other professions, is often not what they actually do in the congregation. Take the case of a plumber. The plumber studies plumbing and fixing pipes and installing water heaters, and then does those things. Clergy, on the other hand, may study ancient languages, philosophy and theology, ethics and Bible, and then find that they must fix pipes and install water heaters! Because this kind of occupational disconnection can lead to a kind of identity crisis, low self-esteem, and profound chronic anxiety, clergy continue to seek outside validation in the form of additional degrees and training. It is not unusual for clergy to have multiple degrees listed on a résumé and a wall full of gilt-edged certificates as a hedge against the chronic anxiety of a job for which no one can agree on the parameters.

When I went to seminary, master's degrees in business administration (MBAs) were popular, then additional clinical pastoral education credits (CPEs), and now a master's degree in family therapy (MFT) is not considered a bad thing. Many clergy seek additional certificates in fund-raising, church growth, or parish management. It is now possible to earn a summer school certificate, suitable for framing, in spiritual direction; this certificate is not awarded by an academic institution but by a monastic order. An entire cottage industry has sprung up around consulting. Clergy mailboxes are filled with letters offering to teach a skill that clergy "must have" for their life and ministry. There are consultants for church growth, consultants for healthy congregations, consultants for small-group workshops, consultants for youth ministry, and so on. Everyone is making money from the clergy's inability to figure out who they are and what they are supposed to be doing. Consultants also prey on the chronic anxiety and insecurity of clergy as they try to minister in a postmodern world.

Edmund Gibbs of Fuller Theological Seminary writes in his book *Church Next: Quantum Changes in How We Do Ministry* that society at large is in the midst of a cultural shift of seismic proportions that affects every area of society.[3] Gibbs notes that the mainline Protestant denominations were formed during the industrial age, a time of slow and incremental change. He goes on to say that the pace of change has now quickened and become more complex. Furthermore, today's change is both discontinuous and chaotic. The priest in the congregation experiences this as anxiety and uncertainty as he or she tries to minister in a world that appears to be out of control and changing with no discernable pattern. Everything appears to be negotiable, nothing appears fixed, and where and when the next change may appear is not readily apparent.

A number of years ago at the Episcopal General Convention, when the use of lay eucharistic ministers was approved, an elderly bishop stood up, pounded his cane upon his desk, and shouted, "What will the clergy do, I ask you, sirs. If we have lay people giving the Eucharist, what will the clergy do?" That same question is still before us today. What will the clergy do? It is my contention that clergy should continue to do that work that has always been the basis of their ministry as clergy, that is, to lead a life of prayer and to lead their congregations in a life of prayer. Historically, the church has been engaged in a variety of cultural and societal ministries and tasks, but a life of prayer remains constant.

Ministering to and with a congregation in this age of change, uncertainty, and chaos requires, I believe, a return to the prayer of the desert fathers and mothers. In the days of the early church, tens of thousands of Christians went into the desert, seeing their work as confronting chaos. But instead of going out into the desert to confront chaos, the priest of today does that in the congregation.

Transforming chaos into constructive and positive energy is the work of a priest. The priest does this by acting as the immune system of the congregation, taking the anxiety of the congregation, the denomination, and society and setting limits and boundaries on how it will affect them. I suggest that it is through the practice of centering prayer that a priest can face the changes in ministry that produce increasing amounts of anxiety found in and generated by the congregation without being overwhelmed. If priests cannot lower their level of reactivity and response then they and their congregations will find the goals that they have set for themselves in ministry impossible to obtain, and their time will be spent in conflict and confusion caused by unresolved anxiety.

The Congregation

In systems theory, the congregation is described as being composed of interlocking family systems. There is the family from which each of us comes, the family that we have now, and the church family as constituted by the congregation. Each family system generates its own positive and negative energy. This energy can be the cause of both chronic and acute anxiety over both real and imagined issues. As I said earlier, chronic anxiety is anxiety that is based on something that might happen but has not happened yet. In a parish, for example, there is a perennial fear among clergy that no one will pledge. If the pledge drive has not begun, the anxiety cannot begin to be alleviated until the drive actually happens. This is a low level of constant anxiety that can lead to a high level of reactivity and response. On the other hand, acute anxiety surfaces when the pledge drive is over and no one has pledged. This acute anxiety is actually easier to handle because there is a real problem, and therefore there might be real solutions.

With chronic anxiety, there is an underlying and almost hidden level of discontent and unease that manifests itself in a variety of content issues. These issues can be centered on the rector's personal traits—she does not smile enough or his children make too much noise in church. Alternatively, these issues might center around professional concerns—his sermons are not very good or her invocation at the city council meeting was thought to be too liberal or too conservative. A sure sign of chronic anxiety is that even if these content issues are resolved, new content issues will spring up in their place. There was a vicar whose congregation complained that he was always involved in a search process and never available to them. In response, he reevaluated his desires and decided to stay forever in that congregation. He announced his intentions to the congregation at a Sunday service. Almost immediately people began to complain about the liberal content of his sermons, about the results of the annual stewardship campaign, about the actions of General Convention, and other issues over which this vicar had no control. Within two months, he and the congregation had separated. It is never the content. It is always the emotional process. In anxious congregations often there will be a string of content issues. When these issues are resolved, another content issue takes its place in a seemingly endless string. Individual problems are solved, but the overall anxiety remains because the underlying process that caused the problems was not addressed.

It is good to remember that the people who make up congregations often come from all parts of society, and bring with them all of their religious as well as secular concerns and issues. This creates in such congregations a highly charged atmosphere filled with all the energy that has not been discharged in the other areas of each church member's life. Often clergy see this energy from the life of individuals discharged in the congregation in terms of conflicts over church polity and practice, life and liturgy, and, on the national level, political issues that often have little to do with life at the congregational level. What once appeared to be a well-defined job whose incumbents typically enjoyed long and sure tenure now seems to have become a high-risk occupation.

THE CLERGY

How is it, then, that the clergy can minister, preach, teach, and heal in this combustible atmosphere? I believe that working in this atmosphere begins with lowering the level of anxiety with each priest acting as the immune system in the congregation in preventing the spread of anxiety. The mechanics for this solution may be found in the service for the "Celebration of a New Ministry."[4] When rectors are installed in their new congregations, presentations are made to them from the members of those congregations and the clergy of that diocese. One of the presentations that is made is a book of prayers, and the clergy person being installed is charged with being among the congregation as a person of prayer. It is by being among the people of the congregation as a person of prayer that clergy are able to transform the hurt, pain, frustrations, and anger that people bring to the congregation from their public and private lives. The clergy can do this by acting as a congregational immune system, taking the anger, pain, hurt, and frustration, and transforming negative and destructive energy into a positive force for ministry.

How the clergy are able to act as immune systems and work with the energy of the congregation through prayer begins with their own interior life. In *Invitation to Love*, Thomas Keating points out that every person begins this life as a helpless infant who is dependent on others to meet such basic needs as food, safety, survival, affection, and esteem.[5] One moment the infant is floating inside the mother's womb in a warm, contained space, where all needs are met, and then in an instant everything changes as the infant is sent out into the world, separated physically from its mother and the solutions to all its needs. Instead of being surrounded by a warm and safe environment, the infant now confronts less dependable forces from the outside. Almost everything is out of the infant's control, and so the child develops appropriate ways of getting its needs met. But no matter how loving a family may be, not all of a child's perceived needs can be met—and certainly not on the timetable the child would like. As a result, a child develops patterns of behavior that it believes will get it what it needs or wants on a timetable of its own choosing. These patterns can then be carried forward into adulthood.

For example, a person deprived of security in childhood may, as a result, seek that security in adulthood. If frustrated in the search to satisfy this need, she or he may react emotionally with grief, anger, jealousy, apathy, and other emotions. Throwing all of your toys out of your crib may attract your parents' attention and get your needs met. When you do the same thing as an adult in your office, throwing the paperwork on your desk out your door, you may get fired. If you are the boss and this is your pattern of behavior, it can cost you valuable workers. Your program for happiness as a child may bring unhappiness as an adult.

Programs for happiness are accompanied by a variety of strong emotions—anger, grief, fear, pride, greed, envy, lust, and apathy—and are felt acutely when the desires for power, control, affection, esteem, and security are frustrated. One of the ways that we can tell when we have hit one of our programmed responses is when we feel intense emotions far in excess of what the situation requires. Strong emotions are replayed like a program on TiVO, tapping into past perceived slights, injustices, and so forth. In one congregation, the vestry made some adjustments in the budget for buildings and grounds. The amount allocated was significantly less than in previous years because of a budget shortfall related to the economy. When the budget was presented at the annual meeting, the chair of the committee responsible for repairs made five impassioned speeches, and his wife made two more, saying ministry was all well and good, but without the building and grounds, there would be no church from which to minister. These pleas were made despite assurances from the vestry before the meeting that any necessary repairs would be made by using reserve funds and that one capital project would be started by using a bank loan. The issue, however, was never the money or its allocation but events in the past life of the chairman of the committee, times when he had felt slighted or ignored. Having his budget read and reduced at a public meeting tapped into all those unsettling emotions, and it resulted in a tirade that had more to do with the past of the committee chair than the present of the congregation.

In order to work with the energies of a congregation and to act as the congregation's immune system, clergy must be conscious of their own programs for happiness and the way that they affect their personal behavior in the present. Clergy need to be aware of their internal drives for power, control, affection, esteem, security, and survival, and to be secure enough not to react to the emotional situations in the congregation that may bring forth these unresolved drives and desires from childhood.

Being aware of these drives alone is not, of course, enough to keep clergy nonreactive and to bring about a fundamental change in the energy of the congregation. Something more is needed. One way to bring about change in the anxiety levels of a congregation and to increase the positive energy levels for ministry is through the practice of centering prayer. Practicing the prayer on a daily basis enables priests and ministers to let go of their own prerecorded programs for happiness—and the difficult emotions that accompany them—relying instead on the security provided by an active relationship with God in prayer. It is through prayer that clergy act as the immune system of the congregation. In a congregation, negative energy can be discharged and transformed through prayer both corporate and private.

Anxiety is nothing more than a form of energy. In small amounts it is positive: it is what causes us to get out of bed in the morning. In larger amounts it can lead to creative drives and advancements in society in all areas from science to art. If we were not anxious as a species, we would have had no reason to change, and, no doubt, we should rapidly have become extinct. In very large doses, however, anxiety can be paralyzing and destructive. I believe it is the work of clergy to transform the energy of the anxiety that people bring to their congregations from their separate families into a form of constructive energy that invigorates both individuals and the community. This is what it means to act as the congregational immune system. The emotional viruses that attack the congregation through the unchecked emotional outbursts of its members or through its struggles to satisfy competing needs are held in check by taking that energy and either quarantining it or returning it to its source.

Individual clergy acting as the immune system, however, can pay a heavy price in both mental and physical health. The toll can be devastating and life-threatening for clergy and also destructive for the congregation. Over a fifty-year history, one congregation rarely kept priests more than three or four years. Often, when the priests left, they did so involuntarily due to substance abuse or improper conduct, and they often left parish ministry entirely. This congregation had been formed from the dissidents of several congregations in one of the Episcopal Church's semigenerational disputes. The anxiety from the issues in their original congregations continued to play out in their relationship with their priest long after the founders of the congregation had died. Many of the priests, who were unable to handle the continuous anxiety, sought to relieve that anxiety in ways that were not healthy. A priest who recently left said that he just could not take it anymore. He had reached a level of anxiety that he could no longer handle, and he felt that his only choice was to leave before he reacted in ways that other ministers in this congregation had done before. He was aware of his situation, but he was still unable to cope with the anxiety.

In order to do the work of ministry in the highly charged atmosphere of the twenty-first-century congregation, clergy need to protect themselves through an *active* contemplative prayer practice. This is important because the priest can be affected by the energies of the congregation in two ways. First, the priest in a congregation is a focal point of a variety of anxious energies and can be easily overcome by the emotional maelstrom in which he or she works. Often this energy is focused through "triangles." Triangles are the basic and most stable unit of human society. The energy between two people is at times too great to be contained within that dual relationship, so a third person is introduced to form a stable relationship. In congregations that third person many times is the minister. Often, the issues raised in a congregational setting can trigger in the minister issues from his or her own life and family. Then, not only do clergy have to work with the congregation as a whole and with the issues of individual members, but they must face past family issues themselves. This often occurs in a congregation when a small incident becomes the flash point for a major congregational battle.

Alternately, it is possible for clergy to work with the energy from anxiety through an active practice of centering prayer. Two twenty-minute periods of prayer each day enable the clergyperson to release the emotional attachments that they may feel to issues being discussed or to the manner in which discussions take place. The clergyperson's work becomes not a matter of siding with one particular group or of winning a particular point but working with the energy of the congregation so that the congregation may begin or continue productive ministry. The practice of centering prayer helps clergy resist reacting to attacks, slights, and innuendoes that may trigger their personal needs for power, control, affection, esteem, security, and survival that are held over from her or his childhood. If we can resist entering into the emotions of the discussions, clergy can be productive in helping a congregation to see their way clear of current emotional turmoil.

In one congregation, the senior warden was to give his annual report. He was in Europe the day before, and his flight back to the United States was cancelled. Being a responsible person, he spent the night in the airport and flew directly home on the first available flight, and then went straight to the church from the airport. He arrived badly jet-lagged and, when he gave his report, he forgot one of the most important vestry proposals of the past year. Immediately, some members of the congregation accused him of trying to conceal vestry actions by editing his report and leaving out this important proposal. He responded with a heated denial. He felt that the members at the meeting were questioning his integrity. There was a potential for this meeting to end in a major parish conflict. The priest was asked for support by both sides. The senior warden wanted the rector to defend him. The rector could have been tempted to give in to his own issues of security and reply, "How dare you attack this fine, hard-working man who was *my* choice for warden!" Rather than respond to his own needs, the rector supported the integrity of his senior warden and noted that more communication would be helpful, and he suggested that further vestry action be postponed until everyone felt that they understood the issues and had an opportunity to express their own opinion.

In this way the priest in this congregation acted as the immune system. He did not participate in the overall level of reactivity, and he did not succumb to his own insecurities around the annual meeting or his choice for senior warden: "My God, if I let this get out of hand, they will want my head next!" He was able to be present and connected but not anxious, even though various church members accused him of bias and collusion. The practice of centering prayer enabled him to be free of his own emotional needs for security, control, power, and esteem. Even though he was worried about the meeting getting out of control, the vestry feeling unsupported by him if he did not take a stand, and the congregation feeling that he was dishonest, the practice of prayer enabled him to bypass his own TiVO buttons, and take the negative energy and anxiety from this conflict and turn it into positive energy for congregational development.

THE PRAYER

Thomas Keating in *Intimacy with God* describes centering prayer as having four distinct moments.[6] The first moment is at the beginning of the prayer when the sacred word is introduced. The sacred word is a symbol of our consent to be present to God and to let God act in our lives. When the sacred word is introduced into the centering prayer practice, we wait in an attitude of expectation for the action of God to take place in our lives. This "action" includes the healing of past emotional hurts that often affect and influence our actions in the present by tapping into past emotional programs, causing us to respond emotionally to them rather than to the present situation.

As thoughts present themselves to us in our prayer we let them fade away, and as this process is repeated we come to the second moment of the prayer, which is deep rest. We sense God's presence in our life and feel a deep interior peace and silence. Many times at this point in prayer this is expressed in feelings of wellness, content, and positiveness. As Julian of Norwich writes in *The Revelations of Divine Love*, "All will be well and every kind of thing will be well," and again, "But all shall be well, and all shall be well, and all manner of thing shall be well." [7] This feeling of wellness characterizes the second moment of the prayer. Each time that the prayer is practiced, this sense of wellness is reinforced, and the person practicing the prayer experiences emotional and physical rest in the presence of God.

This sense of rest and security in the presence of God ushers in the third moment of the prayer, which is that of unloading. In this stage the person practicing the prayer feels secure enough to release the emotional pain and hurt from past life-incidents. Since this pain and hurt left unreleased and self-contained often triggers emotional outbursts in the present, the release of this pain can allow us to be truly present with the congregation in our ministry and not be caught up in the emotions of the moment. The comfort and reassurance that we receive from being in the presence of God allows us to accept the pain being projected by the church members. Rather than react to it, we are free to accept it and then let it go and at the same time let the pain from our own life-experience go also. This emptying is the fourth moment of the prayer.

Having moved through these four distinct movements of the prayer, the person practicing the centering prayer finds herself back at the beginning of the prayer with the sacred word, and the prayer process begins again. Over and over, the practice of accepting and letting go, while secure in the presence of

God and free of past slights, hurts, and traumas, enables us to be truly present for our congregations. By being able to tolerate the emotional pain, we are able to work toward long-term solutions rather than "quick fixes." It is at this point that we are able to act as immune systems for our congregations and even to be healers of persons and institutions. The congregation as body is able to continue with the work that God has called it to do, free of the need to fight or fly. Negative energy is transformed into positive energy through the power of prayer. This is priestly work, and it is the work of the church.

Chapter 8

SEEKING A DEEPER
KNOWLEDGE OF GOD:
Centering Prayer and the Life of a Parish

Tom Macfie

EVERY MONDAY EVENING a dozen people make their way to the church. Half of them are there every week; others come and go as they are able. The group sits in a circle of chairs between the rood screen and the altar. They talk briefly about their lives, read the Gospel for the coming Sunday, and sit in silence for twenty minutes. The purpose of the meeting is for the participants to open themselves to the presence and action of God. On Friday at noon a smaller group gathers for the same purpose: to sit together, to meditate on the Gospel, and to practice centering prayer. Almost all of the participants in the two groups have some form of centering prayer practice that they pursue in solitude during the rest of the week.

At Otey Parish in Sewanee this pattern of prayer is about five years old. It traces its roots back to the commitment of two lay women, Beth Chamberlain and Jennifer Michael, who chose to begin this form of prayer in the life of the congregation. As a priest in this community, and as rector of the parish, I have often pondered the systemic influence of this prayer in the circles that intersect with these two gatherings: the relationships and lives of those who gather for the prayer, the life of this congregation, the community of Sewanee, and the broader church. I would like to offer a few insights on the fascinating interplay that I see between centering prayer and the corporate life of a parish.

I

Centering prayer is a part of the whole in Otey Parish, deeply connected to its eucharistic life and the mission statement of the congregation. A majority of those who practice the prayer attend worship every Sunday. While centering prayer may not be perceived as corporate worship in the usual sense of that phrase, I am struck by the parallels between a support group and the definition of corporate prayer as defined in *The Book of Common Prayer*: "In corporate worship, we unite ourselves with others to acknowledge the holiness of God, to hear God's Word, to offer prayer, and to celebrate the sacraments." [1] As participants go deeper in this form of quiet prayer, they also seem to go deeper in their commitment and devotion to the Sunday celebration of the Holy Eucharist. To judge from their comments, these persons listen with a new ear to the Sunday lectionary, and their awareness of the interplay between the Gospel and the sermon is evident in their questions and reflections on the words of our preachers. One of the most common statements by those who practice the prayer unfolds in a simple way: "The Gospel each Sunday makes more sense because of the readings during the week." Other comments also reveal that something is happening in the hearts of those who practice this prayer: "The words of the liturgy now make more sense." "I know what to do with the times of silence in worship." "I listen more closely to the sermon."

The centrality of the Holy Eucharist and the complementary fruits of centering prayer are also vital in terms of the formal mission statement of Otey Parish. When I arrived in Sewanee in 1997, the congregation had a beautiful mission statement that tied together the baptismal covenant and the mission of the church as expressed on page 855 in the *The Book of Common Prayer* in a fourfold vision: worship, proclamation, service, and education. Unfortunately, the mission statement was underutilized. In the past few years, we have placed more emphasis on the statement by printing it on the cover of the Sunday bulletin, by reciting the statement to begin each gathering of the executive committee and vestry, and by using the phrases in a similar way for weekly staff meetings. The mission statement is no longer buried in a notebook or file; it is part of the fabric of congregational life: "The mission of Otey Parish is to worship God, to proclaim the good news of Jesus Christ, to serve the world for which Christ died, and to educate and nurture our community."

While the mission statement is not part of the format for centering prayer support groups, I suspect that many in those gatherings could talk at length about the way that the statement and the prayer are connected. Participants in the prayer are drawn to the Eucharist; rarely are they pulled away. Many discover a voice for describing the good news, the Gospel, in ways that are unique to their own lives (a good news that many can share with others). Often discussions in the support groups focus on the ways the participants seek to serve in community and personal relationships. I also suspect that many recognize the support that they receive from other participants to be one of the hallmarks of their own nurture and strength in the life of the congregation.

I offer one final observation about our worship. About a year after the first centering prayer group began meeting at Otey, other laypersons took the initiative in saying the daily office, Morning Prayer and Evening Prayer, each day of the week. At one level there are no formal connections between the two. Those who lead the daily office are for the most part not members of the centering prayer support groups. The two practices were not initiated in tandem. They are not offered at the same time of the day. And yet I sense there is a deep connection. The parish is self-consciously a place of prayer. The doors of the church are always open for quiet time and meditation. Fourteen times a week, people will gather to worship in the sanctuary, and, through it all, centering prayer has some fundamental part. A new form of prayer casts its weight in support of the most traditional aspects of worship in the Anglican tradition: "The Holy Eucharist, the principal act of Christian worship on the Lord's Day ... and Daily and Evening Prayer ... are the regular services appointed for worship in this Church." [2] Centering prayer strengthens the fabric of our traditional Christian worship.

II

As we discussed the Gospel one Friday afternoon, one of the participants said, "I can't believe I'm saying this, but I used to find the Bible pretty boring. Now I realize I could spend years on a single passage, and a lifetime exploring scripture." There was no melodrama or remorse, merely a clear statement of what was happening to him as he delved for the first time into the depths of scripture.

The pattern for engaging scripture in the support group is quite simple. Participants read the Gospel for the next Sunday either silently or aloud. The leader of the group asks everyone to offer a word or phrase that holds his or her attention. This takes place with no cross-talk (each person merely offers a word or phrase without responding to the statement of others). After a period of silence, the group reads the passage again, and then follows a discussion that revolves around the following questions: What is the importance of this passage in our corporate life? What is the significance of this passage in your own life? The conversation then becomes more open-ended, and participants often will make connections between their own words and those of others in the group. (One remarkable aside: In five years of centering prayer support groups, I have never heard an argument that takes on that unspoken tone of persons insisting that they are right at the expense of others. One could make a strong argument for the ongoing work of the Holy Spirit merely by noting the way that members of these gatherings feel empowered to speak their minds about God's word while also offering others the opportunity to explore *their* voices engaging the pages of the Bible.) This pattern of reading scripture has spread to other gatherings: staff meetings, vestry meetings, a Sunday class. The Sunday adult class that studies scripture takes a somewhat more traditional approach to Bible study, but the result is the same, a steady engagement with scripture in the life of the local congregation. Each week, on no less than four occasions, and often more, gatherings in the life of the parish are reading and praying the sacred texts that form the heart of the Sunday Eucharist. It is no exaggeration to say that the Gospel for each Sunday becomes part of the daily discourse of parish life, God's people immersed in the corporate and personal encounter with Jesus Christ as revealed in the words of scripture.

III

One of the most fascinating aspects of centering prayer relates to the type of person drawn to the discipline. I am suspicious of statements that begin, "The world is divided into two types of people ... ," but on this occasion, I will risk it. The division in terms of centering prayer would go something like this: half of the people who pursue the prayer are part of the heart and soul of this parish; half who pursue the prayer are seekers.

In the first group, I recognize those who join others in carrying forward the mission and ministry of the church at every level of its institutional life: vestry members, catechists, staff members, chairs of committees, delegates to convention, leaders in outreach. And yet these people seem to have a good balance when it comes to their work in the church. They will say "no" as many times as they say "yes" to new responsibilities, often with a clear sense of why they are moving toward or away from a particular ministry. They seem to know when they need a break. They take care of themselves. The discipline of centering prayer is a way of self-care for some of the most vital leaders in our congregation.

The second group that is drawn to centering prayer wants something. Sometimes, with a certain level of irony, I think they are surprised to find themselves drawn to any manifestation of the institutional church. A good many people in centering prayer have been burned by the church along the way, and the support groups often give them a way to reengage. Some are suspicious of the church, but the warmth of the gathering and the lack of rigid dogma provide them a place to be honest when they ask hard questions. For some individuals the support group has been the avenue to reconnect with the church. It has been the way that has led them—to their own surprise—to a fuller participation in the life of the church. The journey often goes by stages: centering prayer, a fascination with the Eucharist, and then even deeper marks of engagement.

IV

At a personal level the most intriguing influence of centering prayer relates to the outreach of the parish and our efforts to respond to the poor. Otey Parish has long sustained a commitment to social justice and issues of economic and social equality. In 1962, under the leadership of the Reverend David Yates, the parish became the first congregation in Tennessee to integrate all aspects of parish life. (One of the great stories in the history of Otey Parish relates to a parent's conversation with a child on the day that the local elementary school integrated, an event that took place a few years after the integration of the parish. The mother, eager for a response from her child, asked, "Were there any new children at school today?" The child responded, "Just the kids who've been coming to church.") In 1974, under the leadership of Marilyn Powell, the parish formed the Community Action Committee (CAC), a ministry of relief and advocacy for the poor. For over twenty-five years there has been a close relationship between the parish and the Sewanee chapter of the Episcopal Peace Fellowship. I would argue, however, that at times there has been a split between contemplation and social action in the history of the parish. Although technically not opposed to one another, the two have not often been identified as soulmates. In this particular case, a new relationship between these two causes, these two movements in the church, reveals itself most keenly in the story of one particular parishioner, one who was drawn toward centering prayer and working with the poor.

One of the early participants in both centering prayer groups was a woman named Laura Willis. She came to centering prayer as a way to make sense of her own vocational discernment as she moved from a full-time position in university development to the role of a fulltime mother, seeking to balance that important work with concerns related to the community. Through her work in centering prayer, Laura sensed a deep call to work with persons in need, and in January 2001 she was hired as the director of the Community Action Committee. In the past three years the outreach of CAC has multiplied tenfold with increased aid to persons in need, a grant program named the Lifetime Improvement Fund (designed to assist families making systemic changes in their conditions), and the designation of Otey Parish as a distribution center for Second Harvest, a nationwide program providing food for persons in need. As one of the leading advocates in the community for the concerns of the poor, Willis traces the heart and soul of her work to her participation in the Eucharist and the discipline of centering prayer. She herself is challenged to describe how these matters are related: "What I am now trying to discern is how my practice feeds my ministry and how my ministry feeds my practice. I ponder often how they are bound and linked together." In a sense this is a challenge for many who practice centering prayer: How are prayer and action related? The question will never be answered with complete clarity, and yet, at a deep level, many know they are pursuing a line of inquiry that is of profound importance.

V

I offer a note on controversy and then a few concluding remarks. Like almost every congregation in the Episcopal Church, Otey Parish has entered the debates and conversations on the matter of human sexuality. The topic has been discussed in vestry meetings, in gatherings of the adult forum (one of our central avenues for adult education), in sermons, and in private conversations. We experience divergent opinions about the issues that are before us. At the same time, as it happens, we are delving into other controversial topics, or, at least, matters that could easily become divisive: the renovation of the interior of the church, liturgical change, a major capital campaign in the midst of challenging economic times, and the constant evaluation of program initiatives, program staff, and program budgets. What continues to astound me is the way that we are able to focus on the issues that are before us with vigor and vitality, often with divergent views, while not focusing on individuals. We seem to be able to attack the problems and challenges before us without attacking one another. My intuition—and I claim no more for it than that—is that the contemplative practices of many leaders, along with the disciplined prayer lives of others in our congregation, contribute to this process of health and wholeness.

VI

At some level I suspect that everyone who experiments with centering prayer comes to the discipline because of a deep personal need. Perhaps it would be more accurate to call that need "hunger." I began centering prayer eight years ago in order to survive. In the midst of an ordained ministry that bears a good many marks of what the world calls "success," I have known places of despair, and those lonely places called for a response more substantive than additional programs in the life of the church or steady streams of complaint to family and friends. In the mid-1990s, moving through the season of Epiphany, that time when the church speaks of light and glory but the days can be short and dark, I began this journey toward God in the presence of deafening silence. Now it has become part of the fabric of my life, taking its place with the rounds of daily life with my beloved wife and son, the rhythms of the church year and the Sunday Eucharist, the cycles of nature in a place where those marks can still be seen, the pages of scripture that continue to burst with meaning, the rich traditions of the daily office, and all the challenges of ordained ministry in the twenty-first century. Centering prayer takes me to deeper places. It takes me into encounters with those who have gone before me.

I find no better way to conclude these thoughts than to reflect on the words of nineteenth-century theologian William Porcher DuBose, whose description of Christian life bears much in common with the journey of faith that might have included the discipline of centering prayer:

> My proof, I may say my verification, of the fact of God's coming to me, apart from all mystery of the way, may be expressed in this simple truth of experience, that in finding God I found myself: a man's own self, when he has once truly come to himself, is his best and only experimental proof of God. The act of the Prodigal's "coming to himself" was also that of his arising and returning to his Father. [3]

I hope that I may continue to arise, to return, and to know the nature of my life in Christ made real by the Eucharist, the life of a parish, and the varied rhythms of prayer, including this discipline of silence and solitude. I hope others continue to make their own journey home.

Chapter 9

SPIRITUALITY, CONTEMPLATION, AND TRANSFORMATION: *An Opportunity for the Episcopal Church*

Thomas R. Ward, Jr.

"SPIRITUALITY," "CONTEMPLATION," AND "transformation" present a problem and an opportunity for the Episcopal Church. "Spirituality" is used so variously and indiscriminately that it often needs to be defined in any given context so that its meaning is clear, and yet this word points to the heart of our faith. "Contemplation" does not appear in scripture or in *The Book of Common Prayer*, and many Episcopalians thus have no conceptual frame of reference when they hear this word. But "contemplation" was seen to be the goal of the Christian life for most of the church's history. [1] "Transformation" does have roots in scripture and our tradition, but as with "spirituality," "transformation" has been deracinated from its soil in the life of the church. It is used in many different ways. This chapter will attempt to see these words in light of the larger Anglican tradition and to suggest a way that a transformative contemplative spirituality might find a home in the Episcopal Church in our day.

SPIRITUALITY

The Christian West is in the midst of a spiritual revival. The language of spirituality abounds. Retreat centers are full. The Dalai Lama is in high demand as a speaker, as is Thomas Keating. The Paulist Press series titled *Classics of Western Spirituality* is making available texts from the tradition that few laity have known before; many are buying and reading them. These are among the signs of our times.

This revival offers the Episcopal Church a rare opportunity. We see ourselves as part of catholic Christianity, claiming the heritage of the first sixteen hundred years of the church's life, including Eastern Orthodoxy, as well as that of the Reformation. Our understanding of "spirituality" is, therefore, not limited to current use but rather draws on centuries of deep corporate and individual prayer.

While the word "spirituality" is used in many different ways in our day, all Christian spirituality begins with the third person of the Trinity. It is the Holy Spirit who pours God's love into our hearts

(Rom. 5:5). The Spirit of God dwells in us (Rom. 8:9). The Spirit empowers us to enter into the prayer of Jesus, crying "Abba! Father," and thereby bearing witness that we are children of God (Rom. 8:5–6). So we are brought into the very life of the Trinity.

Once in a question-and-answer session at a centering prayer retreat held at St. Benedict's Monastery in Snowmass, Colorado, Thomas Keating said, "The whole of the holy and blessed Trinity dwells within us." I found that statement more than I could digest, and so I asked Father Keating to say more about it. He looked at me and said, "The whole of the holy and blessed Trinity dwells within us." I felt like Nicodemus must have felt when Jesus said to him, "Are you a teacher of Israel, and yet you do not understand these things" (see John 3:10). Here I was, an Episcopal priest of many years standing, and I could not fathom that the Trinity dwelt within me and everyone else.

Later I discovered an essay in which Keating made his point even more emphatically:

> The fundamental theological principle of the spiritual journey is the Divine Indwelling. The Trinity is present within us as the source of our being at every level. Each level of our being—from the most physical to the most spiritual—is sustained by the divine presence.... The Divine Indwelling of the Holy Trinity is a truth of faith that is easily forgotten or avoided.

Yet it is the one on which a radical personal conversion depends. [2]

I am not alone in my initial surprise in hearing that the Trinity dwells within us. In fact, such disbelief is more the norm in our culture than the exception. Take, for instance, some lines from an often-anthologized poem by Robert Frost, perhaps the most popular American poet of the preceding century. The persona of the poem is riding past a field during a fast-falling snow. He sees only a few weeds and no animals. He finds himself in accord with his surroundings:

> I am too absent-spirited to count;
> The loneliness includes me unawares.
>
> And lonely as it is, that loneliness
> Will be more lonely ere it will be less—
> A blanker whiteness of benighted snow
> With no expression, nothing to express.
>
> They cannot scare me with their empty spaces
> Between stars—on stars where no human race is.
> I have it in me so much nearer home
> To scare myself with my own desert places. [3]

It may be that such existential loneliness is behind the spiritual hunger of our day. The god of the enlightenment project—the clock-maker god who set the universe in motion and then abandoned it to wind down on its own—is no longer perceived to be "out there" somewhere. We now send spaceships into outer space, and they bring back no evidence of life as we know it, not to mention "god." Even more disconcerting is the emptiness that we feel within. Is it any wonder that twenty-first-century Americans seek to fill this emptiness with addictive substances, food, sex, and various experiences to which the word "spiritual" is attached? Nor should it surprise us that compensatory twelve-step programs designed to free us from our addictions should also be called "spiritual."

Returning to the Christian perspective, Anglican spirituality traditionally begins with corporate worship: at least weekly reception of the Eucharist on the Lord's Day and daily morning and evening prayer are normative. Personal or private prayer is, at one level, a misnomer. When one goes into one's room and shuts the door and prays to one's Abba in secret, one goes as a member of the mystical Body of Christ, the communion of saints. So, in one sense, this prayer is seen to be an extension of corporate worship. But in another sense it is a category of its own and is acknowledged at such. At the very least, corporate worship gives shape to private prayer.

For many twenty-first-century Christians, including Episcopalians, corporate worship has become rote and sterile. It no longer touches the inner life.

Wade Clark Roof, a noted religious sociologist, puts it this way:

> A…problem for contemporary religious consciousness is the reification of the religious. When the institutional forms of religion become fixed, objective entities—that is, abstracted as a belief system or somehow set apart from the everyday world, as has happened in the Western tradition—there is a real danger that they will get cut off from the inner meanings and feelings that gave them life to begin with. Religion risks losing its subjective and experiential qualities, thus becoming ritually dry and unmoving.
>
> The word "religion" derives from the Latin *religio*, which historically was used in a variety of ways: to designate a greater than human power, to refer to the *feelings* that people have in responding to such power, and to the *ritual acts* by which people expressed their awe and respect in relation to such power. In every instance, as Wilfred Cantwell Smith points out, *religio* embraced the human capacity to perceive meaning and design in life, "to see, to feel, to act in terms of a transcendent dimension." [4]

We can hear in this quotation the roots of the dichotomy between "religion" on the one hand and "spirituality" on the other. "Religion" is the objective, corporate, institutional carrier of a tradition. It runs the risk of becoming a fixed, objective entity, a belief system set apart from the everyday world. From this perspective "spirituality" is the subjective, experiential quality open to a greater than human power; it involves the human capacity to respond to a transcendent dimension in life. This dichotomy lies behind the contrast in the quotation from my first essay in this book:

> "I'm really not religious, at least not in any institutional sense," students often say to me. Then they add, with varying degrees of urgency, "But I have a strong commitment to spirituality." [5]

If religion can go bad in the way mentioned above, this understanding of spirituality can go bad in another way. It can become fixated on experience for experience's sake without attending to the character of the experience. Drug trips, aromatherapy, and sweat-lodge sessions are all associated with one form of spirituality or another, as are Zen meditation and Christian contemplation. If our religious rituals cry out for spiritual renewal, our spiritual experiences need grounding in a tradition.

Perhaps those who design and lead corporate worship should attend to this need for subjective connection, but the worshiper also has a responsibility here. Worship does not begin when we enter the church door and end when we leave. It is a way of life. And personal prayer is at the center of this way of life. A worshiper who only begins to pray when she enters church on Sunday is more likely to find the service "cut off from inner feelings and meanings" than one who has a faithful daily practice of personal prayer. It also helps to be grounded in a corporate tradition of prayer that bears witness to what Keating calls "the Divine Indwelling." I am more likely to flee the inner journey of personal prayer if I believe that I am finally empty inside than I am if I believe that I am in relation to the God who breathes the Spirit of Jesus in my soul, the God who is one in three and three in one.

CONTEMPLATION

> Religion always tends to lose its inner consistency and its supernatural truth when it lacks the fervor of contemplation.... The most important need in the Christian world today is this inner truth nourished by this spirit of contemplation. [6]

Here Thomas Merton agrees with Wade Clark Roof that the collective forms of religion tend to lose their life when they are cut off from an inner quality that Merton calls "contemplation." But what is contemplation? And what is its relation to Anglicanism?

Merton's use of "contemplation" differs from the definitions found in most standard dictionaries. It emerges from a particular strand of monastic prayer that has been lost to much of Western Christianity for almost four hundred years.⁷ This tradition is behind the growing centering prayer movement that is deepening the prayer of so many today.

Thomas Keating traces the history of this tradition in the third chapter of *Open Mind, Open Heart*. The following passage focuses on a central period:

> The Greek Fathers, especially Clement of Alexandria, Origen, and Gregory of Nyssa, borrowed from the Neoplatonists the term *theoria*. This originally meant the intellectual vision of truth, which the Greek philosophers regarded as the supreme activity of the person of wisdom. To this technical term the Fathers added the meaning of the Hebrew *da'ath*, that is, the kind of experiential knowledge that comes through love. It was with this expanded understanding of the term that *theoria* was translated into the Latin *contemplatio* and handed down to us in the Christian tradition.
>
> This tradition was summed up by Gregory the Great at the end of the Sixth Century when he described contemplation as the knowledge of God that is impregnated with love. For Gregory, contemplation is the fruit of reflection on the word of God in scripture and at the same time a gift of God. It is a *resting* in God. In this resting or stillness the mind and heart are not actively seeking him but are beginning to experience, to taste, what they have been seeking. This places them in a state of tranquility and profound interior peace.

This state is not the suspension of all action, but the mingling of a few simple acts of will to sustain one's attention to God with the loving experience of God's presence. [8]

This passage gives us the etymology and history of this use of "contemplation," but it also describes something of the experience as well. Resting, stillness, taste, tranquility, interior peace, and loving experience. Contemplation is finally not so much an intellectual idea as it is an experienced relationship with the Trinity who dwells within the one praying as well as in the external world.

Liturgical worship is the context for this relationship. Monks would participate in the liturgical office, which they called "the Work of God"; then they might remain following the office to continue their prayer. The Rule of Benedict makes special provision:

When the Work of God [the liturgical office] is finished, let all go out in deep silence, and let reverence for God be observed, so that any brother who wished to pray privately may not be hindered by another's misbehavior. And at other times also, if anyone wished to pray secretly, let him just go in and pray not in a loud voice but with tears and fervor of heart. [9]

Over time this individual way of praying in secret became somewhat formalized in a process that became known as *lectio divina*.

Basil Pennington, a contemporary Cistercian and colleague of Thomas Keating, describes this process:

> *Lectio* ... means the reception of the revelation.... For us today, our personal time with the Word of Life, with the Sacred Scriptures, is of primary importance. But we also receive this word through the ministry of others, through their reading, and above all through the Liturgy of the Word....
>
> Again, with *meditatio*.... In the early monastic tradition, meditation involved primarily a repetition of the word of revelation.... The word...was quietly repeated over and over again, even with the lips.... In time, the repetition would tend to interiorize and simplify the word, as its meaning was assimilated.... The Fathers liked to use the image of the cow or other "clean animals who chew the cud." ... As we assimilate them [the words of revelation] through meditation, our whole being comes to respond to them....
>
> Next...we turn to *oratio*, to prayer, to response. When God, the loving Creator and Redeemer so reveals Himself, and we really hear that revelation, that Word of Life, we respond with confident assent, with expressed need, with gratitude, with love. This response is prayer....
>
> Our response grows. It is constantly nourished by illuminating grace. There are moments and seasons of special light. And

it is at these times, which eventually become all times, that the Reality becomes so real to us that a word or a movement of the heart can no longer adequately respond to it. Our whole being must say "yes." This is *contemplatio*. [10]

Lectio, *meditatio*, *oratio*, *contemplatio*—these are the four steps or stages of *lectio divina*, as traditionally understood.

Thomas Keating warns us against treating these four steps in a sequential, mechanical fashion:

[Monks] would start reading the scripture [*lectio*] and when something struck them, they would stop, reflect on the text, and then pray over it, asking God for the good things they read about. They would move from discursive meditation [*meditatio*] to affective prayer or aspirations of the will [*oratio*], then to repeating the same aspiration over and over again, and finally they would experience resting in God [*contemplatio*]. This was the goal of the whole process.... They would also read very slowly, the whole process of *lectio* taking at times a couple of hours. [11]

So one description of this understanding of "contemplation" is "resting in God." Keating also gives another one-sentence description: "Contemplative prayer is a process of interior transformation, a conversation initiated by God and leading, if we consent, to divine union." [12]

When Keating and those who work with him introduced contemplative prayer to contemporary laity, they did not start with the full process of *lectio divina*.[13] They knew that two hours was more than most people could or would give. So they eliminated the first three moves and went directly to *contemplatio*. Interestingly, as the centering prayer movement[14] has evolved, many of those who have developed a faithful practice of centering prayer have also begun to seek the roots of contemplation in *lectio*. There are now workshops in *lectio divina* that complement those in centering prayer. It is as if the Spirit moves the one praying to recapitulate the process. Here is Keating's observation:

> I am convinced that one can begin *lectio* at any one of the four stages—reading, reflecting, responding, or resting. In fact, some are better off beginning with resting in God [*contemplatio*] precisely because of our cultural conditioning. *Lectio* is a dynamic process; that's why we emphasize its nature as relationship. The relationship quality of centering prayer implies all four levels. If one does not have the first three stages of *lectio* worked into one's psyche, centering prayer will gently attract the practitioner to go back and fill in the space. Centering prayer will lead one back to the earlier stages of *lectio* because they are an integral part of the whole organic process.[15]

What is the distinction between contemplative prayer on the one hand and centering prayer on the other? And why do Thomas Keating and those who work with him emphasize the distinction? Keating calls centering prayer both a prayer and a method. In doing so he emphasizes that the method is in the service of one's relationship to God. Centering prayer is not a technique. It is a way of preparing for the gift of contemplation. [16] He reserves the word "contemplation" itself for the stage of prayer that is a "pure gift of the Spirit." [17] Centering prayer focuses on what the one praying does; contemplation focuses on what God does. John of the Cross calls contemplation "a loving inflow of God, which, if not hampered, fires the soul in the spirit of love." [18]

Earlier I posed the question of the relation between this way of praying and Anglicanism. As a branch of the church with its roots in the Reformation, in the beginning Anglicanism reacted against all things Roman. Henry VIII not only closed monasteries, he confiscated monastic lands. But in earlier days, England was fertile ground for contemplation. The fourteenth century was particuarly fruitful. In fact, *The Cloud of Unknowing*, a fourteenth-century work by an anonymous monk, is the proximate source of centering prayer. Consider this passage:

> Thought cannot comprehend God. And so, I prefer to abandon all I can know, choosing

rather to love him whom I cannot know.
Though we cannot know him we can love
him. By love he may be touched and embraced,
never by thought. Of course, we do well at
times to ponder God's majesty or kindness
for the insight these meditations may bring.
But in the real contemplative work you must
set all this aside and cover it with a cloud
of forgetting. Then let your loving desire,
gracious and devout, step bravely and joyfully
beyond it....

So whenever you feel drawn by grace to this
contemplative work and are determined to do
it, simply raise your heart to God with a gentle
stirring of love.... A naked intent toward God,
the desire for him alone, is enough.

If you want to gather all your desire into one
simple word that the mind can easily retain,
choose a short word rather than a long one.
A one-syllable word such as "God" or "love"
is best. But choose one that is meaningful to
you.... Use it to beat upon the cloud of darkness
above you and to subdue all distractions. [19]

Nothing like this passage occurs in Anglicanism
after the Reformation, although there are traces of
the contemplative spirit in such writers as Richard
Hooker, George Herbert, and Thomas Traherne.
And from the formative years of Anglicanism there
has been an Anglo-Catholic movement that has
had within it the seeds of contemplation. But it is in
The Book of Common Prayer itself that those seeds

are most deeply planted. Thomas Cranmer edited
and combined the Benedictine monastic offices into
morning and evening prayer. In this way prayerful attending to the reading of scripture has been
retained in principle, and this has kept alive the
spirit of *lectio divina*. (We notice it in particular
in the Collect for Proper 28. It refers to the Holy
Scriptures and asks that we might "read, mark,
learn, and *inwardly digest* them." [20] My emphasis.)
One point of this chapter is to encourage congregations to offer the office publicly and to exhort individuals to pray it wherever they are.

In offering centering prayer workshops in
Episcopal congregations I have found it useful to
begin with the section on prayer and worship in
The Book of Common Prayer (pages 856–857).
It gives the group some common language and
grounds us in our own tradition. While the word
"contemplation" is not used in this section, seven
different kinds of prayer are listed—from thanksgiving to petition. Two kinds, in particular, help us
make the connection to contemplation. Adoration
is described as "the lifting up of the heart and mind
to God, asking nothing but to enjoy God's presence." Praise: "We praise God not to obtain anything, but because God's being draws praise from
us." Both adoration and praise emphasize God's
action in prayer and minimize the activity of the
one praying. It is also helpful to have the Catechism

state that there is a wordless way of praying, that all Christian prayer is Trinitarian, and that prayer is always responding to God. (We do not initiate this relationship.) This last point is consistent with the Catechism's emphasis on the biblical theme of covenant. ("A relationship initiated by God to which a body of people respond in faith.")[21] Our contemporary form of Anglicanism has a basis for fostering contemplation.

I began this section with a quotation from Thomas Merton that points to the need for the revival of a spirit of contemplation so that religion might regain its inner consistency and supernatural truth. That followed a quotation from Wade Clark Roof that described contemporary public worship as cut off from the inner feelings and meanings that gave such worship life to begin with. But worship that is truly alive—whether it is corporate or private—has the effect of transforming the worshiper who, in turn, is called to be God's servant in transforming the world.

TRANSFORMATION

Contemplation is not only an end in itself but also a means to the end of the transformation of the one praying. And this, in turn, is not just an end in itself but a means to the end of the one praying being an agent of transformation in God's world. Just as there is a tension in the tradition between liturgical and individual prayer, there is also a tension between contemplation and action. Most often this is a false dichotomy: those who pray are called to action, and all who act are called to prayer so that their deeds may be grounded in God.

In Romans 12:2, Paul turns from proclaiming the Gospel in the first eleven chapters to applying what he proclaims to daily life. It is the move from *kerygma* to ethics. It is as if he says, "God has transformed the world in Christ. Be transformed, and be agents of transformation" (cf. 2 Cor. 5:18–20). We begin this process in our baptisms where we are buried and united with Christ in his death and empowered by his resurrection to walk in newness of life (Rom. 6:3–5). But there is another tension here: between what God has already done once and for all, what God continues to do, and what God calls us to do in response. On the one hand, God has conquered sin; on the other, God calls on us to complete this work by our prayer and action. We see this tension and incompleteness most clearly in Romans 7:

> I can will what is right, but I cannot do it. For I do not do the good that I want, but the evil I do not want is what I do. Now if I do what I do not want, it is no longer I that do it, but sin that dwells within me. (18b–19)

In Romans 6:6 Paul refers to this self enslaved to sin as "our old self," and he exhorts his readers to another way of life. But in this passage Paul never makes explicit that there is a "new self" that emerges through baptism. However, in Ephesians 4:22–24 the author balances the old with the new. It is through our participation in the sacramental life of the church, through our personal prayer, and through our action in the world that we are to continue to move from the old to the new self. By our participation in the Eucharist, in particular, we continue our transformation. Moreover, in our day many are called to extend their participation in the Eucharist and deepen their relation with the Trinitarian God through contemplative prayer.

In describing this deepening, Thomas Keating translates the Pauline language of the old and new selves into what he calls the false self and the true self. He writes that in baptism the false self is ritually put to death and the true self comes to birth.[22] The true self is made in the image and likeness of God. To be sure, our participation in the Eucharist nurtures this new life in us, but Keating says that we need a daily practice of contemplation to further this growth. He writes:

> We can bring our false self to liturgy and to the reception of the sacraments, but we cannot bring the false self forever to contemplative

prayer because it is the nature of contemplative prayer to dissolve it. [23]

How does this occur? Keating uses contemporary
psychology as a handmaid to explain the false and
true selves and the process of moving from the one
to the other through contemplation.

For Keating, "*original sin* is a way of describing
the human condition, which is the universal experience of coming to full reflective self-conscious-
ness without the certitude of personal union with
God." [24] The "desert places" that Frost describes
in his poem, quoted above, are the consequences
of such deprivation. Keating calls them "our intimate sense of incompletion, dividedness, isolation,
and guilt." [25] He says that we unconsciously form
our false selves to defend our being from "harm
that other people have done to us knowingly or
unknowingly at an age when we could not defend
ourselves." [26] But beneath the defensive structure of
our false selves is the true self, the self made in the
image and likeness of God.

Contemplative prayer dissolves the false self by
healing the emotional wounds of our unconscious.
When Paul says that he can will what is right but
that he cannot do it, he is bearing witness to the
power of sin beneath the level of consciousness. For
us to be healed, the will is necessary but not sufficient. In centering prayer we consent to God's presence and action within us; in this way we use our

conscious minds to open to the Spirit who heals the wounds deep in our unconscious.

Keating compares the practice of contemplative prayer to the experience of psychotherapy. Here the Risen Christ dwelling within is the Divine Therapist, and the one praying is the patient. Times of prayer are therapeutic sessions. The patient enters into a transference relation to the Risen One, and through this relation the emotional wounds of a lifetime are healed. The false self is deconstructed. The barriers that keep us from being our true selves are removed, and we become God's loving presence in the world. [27] Keating writes about this transformation through prayer: "Do it [centering prayer]! It will then do you." [28] In both psychotherapy and contemplation it is the loving relationship that heals.

As paradoxical as it sounds and is, the one praying experiences the fruits of the Spirit not so much in the time of prayer as in her life in the world. Most often a spouse or other close friend notices differences in behavior before the one practicing this prayer does. The Spirit works from inside the psyche outward and in relation to those closest to the one praying rather than those more remote, particularly at first. [29]

I discovered this prayer (or it discovered me) while I was on sabbatical in 1988. I came back to my home, and my wife soon mentioned the difference she noticed in me. She asked, "What are you doing differently down there," referring to my study where I prayed? She said, "You used to come out as angry as when you went in. But now you're different. You're easier to live with." I was surprised. I did not know that I was so difficult to live with before, and I was not aware of any change in my affect or behavior. [See, for instance, Chapter Three, pp. 67–68 —ED.]

I began to teach this prayer in the parish I was serving. A significant minority of the parish joined me, and they began to notice changes in their lives as well. In particular, two groups were represented in significant numbers: those doing hands-on outreach and those participating in lay pastoral care (the Stephen Series). Those doing outreach needed spiritual nourishment so that they could continue their good work with God's poor. Those doing pastoral care said that they needed to deepen their own prayer lives so that they could pray more deeply with the people that they were called to serve. There was a reciprocal relationship between centering prayer and deep service: the more one was committed to service, the more one needed to pray, and vice-versa. It is not surprising that Mother Teresa and her nuns practiced contemplative prayer for an hour every day before they headed for the streets of Calcutta to minister to the dying.

Keating teaches that the goal of the Christian life is to live an ordinary life with extraordinary love. The more I practiced this prayer, the more I saw that I had spent most of my life, including all of my ordained life, with an unconscious striving to be extraordinary, fostering what I have come to call "the Tom Ward self-glorification project"—my personal version of the false self! Having access to a practice that undermines that project and makes me more aware of opportunities to serve in the present moment has been and is a great grace. I have also noticed this grace in others.

So contemplation is a means to transformation—for the one praying, for those closest to him, and, by extension, for those furthest away. It empowers the one praying to live a faithful life within the structures of the twenty-first century and to be an agent of transformation in minute ways wherever one finds one's self.

CONCLUSION

Many in our day are seeking a genuine spirituality grounded in centuries of practice. *The Book of Common Prayer*, informed by the church year, offers this, providing a rhythm of worship for each day, each week, each year. It is a way of opening our lives to the presence of God. More particularly, congregations have an opportunity to renew the lives of their parishioners and their communities by publicly offering the daily office as well as the Holy Eucharist at least weekly. At first only a few may participate, but the offering itself encourages those unable to be present to pray where they are. It also provides a scripturally based context for fostering the deeper relationship with God that a contemplative practice makes possible.

Congregations might also offer instruction in private prayer. While personal prayer is always unique to one's own relation with God, the church has almost two millennia of experience, and there are many resources available. Again, many in our day are practicing one form of contemplation or another, both within and outside the church. Some are looking for a congregation that might support what they are finding in the contemplative way. Others might be open to instruction in centering prayer, that first rung on the ladder of contemplation.

Contemplation and the local congregation need one another. In describing the powerful psychic energy that contemplative prayer releases, Keating writes that the one praying needs to be grounded in dedication to God and in service to others.[30] The local congregation has these to offer in corporate worship and in numerous outreach opportunities. In this way contemplative prayer undergirds the many ministries of the congregation by transforming their participants, and those ministries, in turn, provide necessary outlets for action in God's world for those who are being transformed. Contemplative Outreach

offers a way for local congregations to become centers for contemplation and action, for a spirituality
that serves the world in God's name.

Chapter 10

KEEP THE REST:
Practicing Silence while Professing Poetry

Jennifer Michael

When God at first made man,
Having a glass of blessings standing by,
Let us (said he) pour on him all we can:
Let the world's riches, which dispersed lie,
Contract into a span.

So strength first made a way;
Then beauty flow'd, then wisdom, honour,
    pleasure:
When almost all was out, God made a stay,
Perceiving that alone of all his treasure
Rest in the bottom lay.

For if I should (said he)
Bestow this jewel also on my creature,
He would adore his gifts in stead of me,
And rest in Nature, not the God of Nature.
So both should losers be.

Yet let him keep the rest,
But keep them with repining restlessness:
Let him be rich and weary, that at least,
If goodness lead him not, yet weariness
May toss him to my breast.
                    —GEORGE HERBERT, "The Pulley" [1]

I RECENTLY TAUGHT THIS poem for the first time in a poetry course subtitled "Apprehensions of the Sacred." The course is designed to give students a solid grounding in poetic forms, figurative language, and the matter of which poems are made. At the same time, it indulges a desire of my own to try to unite—or at least to understand—two parallel and seemingly contradictory threads in my life: a passion for words and a growing attraction to silence. Naturally, when I begin to talk about the role of centering prayer in my life, a poem comes immediately to mind.

Reading "The Pulley" in the light of my prayer practice, I was struck by the way that Herbert puns on the word "rest"—and by how keenly the closing phrase reflects my own experience. I am often led, not by goodness but by sheer exhaustion, to collapse in God's arms. The poem reminds us how elusive rest can be in our hyperactive world. Indeed, the "richer" we are with wealth, education, family, and other definitions of success—even such true blessings as strength, beauty, and wisdom—the harder it is to *rest*, to release the illusion that we control such things.

While it is true that Americans work longer hours and take far fewer vacations than our European counterparts, the greatest obstacles to rest are often internal. As an academic, I enjoy more "time off" than most people, and I push myself hard to reach the end of each semester, only to find that my brain and body refuse to get the message that it is time to relax. Insomnia, depression, and a vague anxiety often come on the heels of graduation—and my conversations with colleagues indicate that my experience is not unique.

Thomas Keating describes the purpose of centering prayer as our "resting in God." Therein lies the great attraction—and also the greatest challenge of the practice for me.

Until six years ago, I would have been an unlikely candidate for centering prayer. Like Anne Lamott, I grew up believing that "you are what you do." [2] Blessed with a loving, smart, and affluent family, I had no excuse not to perform well. I was further blessed (or cursed) with enough academic success that I assumed a direct relationship between effort and happiness. I graduated from Sewanee and went to Oxford University on a Rhodes scholarship. At age twenty-eight I had my doctorate and my dream job of teaching at my alma mater. Then, at thirty my marriage came apart, and I suddenly found myself on a path without a map. I could not read, write, or think my way out of the wilderness. Worst of all, I somehow thought that I should be able to "handle it." Having spent my life proving how capable I was, it was terrifying to admit how helpless I suddenly felt.

According to John Tarrant, this is a common experience:

> The journey into a life of awareness begins for
> most of us in a moment of helplessness.... Yet
> this unexpected fall is also a gift, not to be
> refused—an initiation ordeal preparing us for
> new life. The enveloping dark strips us of our
> sleepyheadedness, our assumption that who
> we now are and the life we now know will
> be enough. The night is not interested in our
> achievements. [3]

Therapy was (and remains) the first step to learning compassion for myself, and I shall say more about
that later. The other necessary piece was a daily practice. Around this time, Tom Ward, my friend and
our chaplain at All Saints' Chapel in Sewanee, asked
me, "How's your prayer life?" I squirmed, as most
people tend to do under that question. I was raised a
Methodist but became an Episcopalian in graduate
school, drawn to the liturgy and sacraments with
their enactment of Christ's presence in the here and
now. Still, church remained an external involvement,
an "activity" that was not really a part of my inner
life. With the divorce hanging over me like a terrible
failure, I was reluctant to look God in the face. I told
this to Tom, and at his suggestion I went to a one-
day workshop on centering prayer. During my first
sitting I was so overwhelmed with desire—for love,
acceptance, understanding, God—that I said, "This
will never work for me." It was anything but peaceful. I often felt that I was hovering on the edge of one
of those medieval maps of the world with the legend

"Here Be Dragons" just beyond the shore. Still, I kept at it, and before long I was sitting twice a day, not because I thought it would make me a better person but because something in me was nourished by that practice alone.

The priority of this prayer practice in my life became clear over the next several months as my morning routine changed. Initially, I would squeeze in a sit after my morning walk and breakfast. Gradually, the sit moved up in priority, even before coffee, so that the only thing that I did beforehand was to feed the cats (who, by the way, gradually began to "sit" with me in their own way, watching me quizzically from across the room). I arranged my schedule so that I could attend a weekly support group, and eventually became a co-leader of the group. None of this felt like something that I "ought" to do; it was simply where I was led.

After about six months of practice, I attended my first eight-day retreat, which (among other things) freed me from obsessing about certain details of the practice. I found that I knew without looking approximately when twenty minutes were up. I learned that I could focus my intention on the breath rather than a sacred word. Words for me can often be seductive and therefore distracting. I found that insistent trains of thought were often accompanied by tension in some part of the body; if I could relax those muscles, the thought would pass too. Best of all, I discovered that there were two levels of aware-ness: the "river" on which thoughts glide past like boats, and down below it a deep quiet in which the connection to God is unbroken. My attention might waver, but God's does not.

The retreat experience "hooked" me as well, and although I have not managed one every year, I have made three eight-day retreats at St. Mary's Conference Center in Sewanee and one month-long, independent sabbatical retreat at the Desert House of Prayer in Arizona. Each retreat has its own rhythm, but variations on the same theme tend to dominate. I long to feel God's presence in some immediate way, and most of the time what I feel is silence—or my own desperate attempts to fill the void. Thomas Merton says that the true contemplative would rather *not* have proof of God's presence.[4] If he is right, I doubt that I will ever be a true contemplative, but I am gradually learning to trust that God is in the silence and that the void is not one of negation but of letting-be, a space that holds us and allows us to grow. Or, as Mark Jarman puts it:

> Amazing to believe that nothingness
> Surrounds us with delight and lets us be
> . . . .
> This God recedes from every metaphor,
> Turns the hardest data into untruth,
> And fills all blanks with blankness. This love shows
> Itself in absence, which the stars adore.[5]

I mentioned that therapy has been part of my journey. Keating refers to centering prayer as "divine therapy," and indeed the parallels with psychotherapy are striking. The relationship with the therapist helps the client to feel safe enough to feel and express painful emotions, which then lose their toxicity. Keating is also fond of the digestive metaphor, in which we "evacuate" or vomit up the "emotional junk of a lifetime" during the deep rest of prayer.[6] He implies that it is better not to analyze or interpret this junk. We should just flush it away and return to the sacred word.

In my own case this divine therapy and its human counterpart have been complementary. I was blessed to find a therapist who is also a member of the clergy with a history of contemplative practice. What I found in working with him was more than a simple encouragement for my own practice. Before I could begin to trust completely in God's love and acceptance, I needed to feel accepted and understood by another human being, to be able to look into someone's eyes and to know that that person would not look away, no matter what he saw. To me, that is the way God looks at us. As Keating says of Brother Bernie O'Shea, "When someone treats you in such a way that it makes you think of God, that person clearly is a sacrament of God's presence."[7] Such people cannot take the place of God in our lives, but they serve a necessary function as outward and visible signs of God's presence and action among us.

Herbert beautifully describes the welcoming action of this presence: "Love bade me welcome: yet my soul drew back, / Guilty of dust and sin." [8] In this poem the soul, entering heaven, lingers shamefaced on the threshold, unwilling even to look at "Love," or Christ. This "quick-ey'd Love" responds by moving ever closer, smiling, taking the soul's hand, saying, in effect, "Everything about you belongs to me." God does not put up barriers to salvation; we create them ourselves. In the spiritual life, unlike the academic one, I have had to learn the same thing over and over again: "Nothing can separate us from the love of God." I hear it in church every Sunday, and I open myself to it in every sit. In therapy I also keep working to dismantle the false self.

The trouble is that the false self (as it keeps reminding me) is what got me where I am professionally. It thrives on perfectionism, productivity, and praise. So, for instance, before I go on a retreat and for the first few hours I am there, the false self tries to talk me out of it: "What a waste of time! Think of the work you could be doing. You have classes to prepare and articles to write." Or, more subtly: "You don't need this. Your spiritual life is just fine. What you need is a vacation, not a week of sitting in silence with a room full of other zombies." By midweek I manage to send the false self on her own vacation, but she is always back soon after I return to my "real life": "See! You didn't learn very much on that retreat. Look how easily you let things irritate you."

The false self thinks she is responsible for everything. By making herself indispensable, she guarantees her own importance. Academia is more than willing to enable her by putting her on committees, publishing her work (maybe), and keeping lists of what she has accomplished.

Soon after I began centering prayer, I found that my own reactions to professional success were changing. I could be momentarily elated when an article was accepted for publication, but then I remembered, "If you live by that, you die by that." I could no longer let the expectations and judgments of others define me. I continued to pour just as much energy into teaching and scholarship, but my motivations had changed. I realized that I loved teaching primarily for the relationships it fostered, not because I wanted to show how much I knew. I had been showing what I knew for the first thirty years of my life. When I stopped holding the material up as a shield, I instead came to see it as a space in which the students and I could meet. Sometimes they do not want to enter that space; sometimes it is easier for me to let them stay outside and listen to me lecture. Still, I have come to believe, on the best days, that what I offer to students—*who I am*—means more than simply telling them what I know. I only know this because that was what my best teachers did for me.

That conviction, too, easily gets lost in the busyness of the semester. Two years ago I was determined to take a true sabbatical, in defiance of the academic culture that honors the word only in arithmetical terms. I spent part of my semester in the British Library, but I also spent time at the Desert House in Arizona and on the island of Iona. From Iona I brought back a miniature Saint John's cross, a replica of one that stands outside the abbey. I placed it on my desk in the office, beside the computer, to remind me to look at every person who enters as the image of God. By the end of the next academic term, the tiny cross was obscured by piles of papers. The symbolism was apt: despite daily practice, I had lost my focus and needed another retreat to restore it. Rather than berate myself, however, I smiled at this discovery and was grateful for the opportunity to redirect my attention.

Centering prayer has made me a more sensitive reader of my own psyche, and it has also affected the way that I read, write, and understand poetry. During my sabbatical in the desert, my days fell into a natural rhythm of silent prayer, communal worship, walking, reading, and writing. The authors that I read—Blake, Rilke, Merton, Pema Chödrön, David Budbill—led me deeper into silence, into a feeling of gentleness, in which the inside and outside were separated only by a thin membrane. In time, the silence opened up a space inside me for the texts to grow and resonate. One day I was feeling anxious about my lack of progress on my book, and on a walk through one of the desert "washes" (dry riverbeds), I realized that what I was feeling was yet another attempt by my rational mind to control the situation, rather than let God direct my time and energy. At about that time I noticed in the intense sunlight that a tiny piece of glass or quartz in the sand would shine from a great distance. Immediately I thought of Blake's line, "to see a world in a grain of sand," and when I turned again to my chapter on his epic poem "Jerusalem," I understood what he meant about the "jewels of the soul" that become hard and opaque when we fail to enter imaginatively into another person's being. Blake and the desert were both saying something to me about turning vision inside out. For a while at least, I felt that I was understanding Blake from the inside, and my desert walks became a form of primary research.

I am still learning how to integrate words and silence, work and rest, in my everyday life. Clearly, there are countless ways in which "work," thoughtlessly defined as "staying busy," undermines spiritual growth. Work in the holier sense, however, is God's eventual destiny for us. As Belden Lane puts it, "Work is paying attention to what matters most." [9] He might well be speaking of centering prayer. This sacred work is not identical with our job, though ideally the job will make it possible for us to do the work that is not just ours but God's.

Thomas Keating describes the contemplative life as "resting even in the midst of activity. This is to do what God does. God is always at rest and always creating at the same time, and yet beyond both." [10] Merton quotes a similar idea from Peter of Celles: "God works in us while we rest in him." [11] Returning to the sacred word in silence helps me to remember who is really doing the work—and to rest in that work with joy.

Chapter 11

CHANGING YOUR MIND:
*Contemplative Prayer and
Personal Transformation*

Brian C. Taylor

I F ONE STAYS with a practice of meditation or con-templative prayer for more than a short while, it becomes obvious even in the silence of prayer that one's ordinary patterns of thought and emotional reactivity are quite persistent. It also becomes obvious in one's daily life that patterns of behavior, temperament, relationship, and self-image are also persistent. Whatever fantasies we may have had at the beginning of a spiritual practice about meditating (or living) in peaceful holiness—and "letting go" of all that stands in the way of this bliss—these quickly evaporate at the powerful insistence of old habits of mind and emotion that *will not* let go their grip. Over time, we are sometimes even disappointed to discover that our spiritual "awakenings" are only more subtle versions of our lifelong, neurotic habits of being. Control, for instance, wears a spiritual disguise in many people. Real change is difficult and slow. We begin to wonder: Is change possible? If it is possible, how on earth does it take place? Can we actually move from the self-serving drivenness of attachment and aversion to real freedom and openness to life as it presents itself? Can we ever move out of our own conditioned limitations into a new way of being in God?

NEUROLOGY: THE HARDWARE OF OUR INNER LIFE

The brain is the organ that generates habitual mental activity, which in turn keeps us locked into certain patterns of thought and emotion instead of being open to God in the moment. In order to understand how contemplative practice really does change us over time, transforming us into the image of Christ, it may be helpful to look at neurological change and to examine how this takes place within the context of contemplation. For this examination a little basic neurology is necessary, and so a temporary side trip, away from the theological and spiritual language of the contemplative tradition, is needed first. [1]

Powerful habits of being are formed in the brain very early in life. Through genetics and experiential conditioning, very particular neurological pathways are laid down that become our brain's permanent "hardware," on which we then run all of life's "software" of mental and emotional activity, including our efforts to learn and change. Given this biological reality, it certainly is naive to think that we can move out of old habits of mind and heart by reading a book, hearing an inspiring talk, having an insight, or praying once in a while. The good news is that human beings, by the grace of our Creator, are amazingly adaptive and *can* change, even neurologically. One of the ways that we can actually alter our neurology—and therefore our awareness, thinking, feeling, and behaving—is through contemplative prayer.

There is a neurological basis to all of our patterns of thought, emotion, attitude, and mood. This is true even of the habitual traits that we attribute to "personality." As early as our fetal development, genetic influences begin building our brain. Particular neurological pathways are laid down. Then, as soon as we are born, repeated experience further constructs the brain. The earlier, stronger, and more repetitive our experience is, the more these pathways become a part of our brain's hard-wiring. This is why early abuse is so hard to overcome. The damage to self-image becomes a permanent part of our brain's very makeup. While it is possible to learn to use new pathways that contradict, inhibit, and even overwhelm old ones, we can never erase them.

Let us take a closer look at what happens in the formation and ongoing activity of the brain. As

Daniel Alkon describes it, "The brain is a seemingly infinite collection of precisely ordered cells communicating with each other in the language of electrical signals."[2] All of the activity of the brain is stored in the movement of electrical impulses that move in pathways from neuron to neuron. This is true of emotion, thought, habitual attitudes, patterns of relationship, responses to stimuli, and information that is gleaned from both memory and current experience.

We may think of a neuron as a cell that has branches. At one end of the neuron are branches that receive electrical signals from other neurons, called *dendrites*. At the other end are branches that transmit signals to other neurons, called *axons*. When a signal is moving through the neuron, it reaches the terminals at the end of the axon, and if there is a sufficient charge, *neurotransmitter* chemicals are released that flood and move the signal across a space between neurons that is called a *synapse*. *Receptor* chemicals then receive the signal, and move it through the dendrite into its neuron. This activity moves information along familiar, well-worn pathways to various regions of the brain, stimulating thought, sensory awareness, understanding, moods, and action. Billions of these signals, neural connections, and pathways work simultaneously and instantaneously.

One of the amazing things about this activity is that information is not contained within the neurons themselves, like boxes stored in warehouses, but rather in the *interaction* between neurons, in their patterns of relationship. Just as people, ecological systems, subatomic particles and waves, and planets and galaxies exist only in relationship, so it appears that thought, memory, and emotion exist only in movement and interaction. While the brain is still being constructed during infancy and childhood, neurological pathways are being designed through repeated experience and memory that later will be the familiar roads of all thought and emotion. The brain's use of these pathways is a little like cows that graze on hillsides, wearing familiar paths in the side of the hill, unconsciously and automatically following along them.

As it develops, the brain makes associations between new stimuli and memory, arranging experience into familiar patterns. New events, joined together with remembered ones, create maps upon which neural impulses can move. The brain does this by choosing which synaptical connections live or die through repeated use or disuse, thereby determining which neurons are connected. The neurons' branches, their *axons*, actually travel to sites where new synapses are formed; alternately, axons withdraw or degenerate when they fail to join synaptically. The pathways of childhood impressions are thus imprinted in double strength: in network activity and in the brain's very design. In early childhood the basic neurological map is in the process of developing. Once mapped, the mature brain cannot be redesigned. It cannot hardwire itself all over again.

After the brain is essentially constructed, developmental learning takes place within the pathways that are already laid down, like new software that is running on established hardware. From this point on, learning happens by chemical changes that adjust the emphases that are given to particular synaptic connections. Levels of electrical activity in the neurons shift as learning takes place, and different synapses are thereby emphasized and new routes are learned. Through the strengthening or weakening of neural connections, learning alters the effectiveness of various pathways.

In addition to this process of emphasis, or *weighting*, neurons actually sprout new branches (dendrites and axons) that reach out for new connections. This neural process of development is called *arborizing*. So it is that, as we learn, we work chemically within the existing pathways. Activity may change as we learn, but not basic structure. The brain's "ground rules" of structure and pathways stay the same, and all new learning happens within these rules.

This is why change is so difficult. In order to change we must *weight* neurons and synapses differently, and we must *arborize* new connections. This takes time and, above all, repeated experience. The brain only learns through repetition. However, if new experiences are strong and repetitive enough, they *will* alter our habits of mind, emotion, and behavior. That is the good news!

RESISTANCE TO CHANGE

Powerful forces, however, are at work to hinder the process of real change. Even our personal attributes— of optimism or gloominess, openness to or suspicion of others, and a host of other traits—are imbedded in billions of neurons, in their very structural connections. This is also true of our core beliefs, our life-story as we perceive it to be, which is the way we see life and our selves in relation to it.

When I use the term *core belief*, I am not speaking of one's core values and religious beliefs, but rather those understandings of one's self and the world that are born out of early experiences. Many of these experiences, and elements of our core beliefs as well, can be healthy and holy, such as an early experience of love and a lifelong understanding that we are loveable and can trust the world. My concern, however, is how we might work with God to uncover and be freed from core beliefs that are self-limiting and destructive. Because we are complex and imperfect beings, we share these patterns as well as more benign ones.

If, for instance, we learned a core belief in childhood that life is dangerous and that we are a victim, it will take very patient and powerful neurological work to become free from this belief. The story itself is imbedded in countless connections, even in the very map of the brain. Particular circumstantial stimuli originally taught us this belief, and every time these stimuli reoccurred in early childhood, that particular perspective was reinforced.

Over the years, as new but seemingly related stimuli come our way, we make and record even more associations within the same neural pathways. The patterns become stronger. A person betrays us, and this experience reinforces existing links. Our core beliefs become more ingrained; we become more determined to respond to stimuli in patterned ways, even when original events have passed from memory. Neurological pathways not only remain intact, they remain active, creating new reinforcements out of current experience. This is why we keep finding ourselves in the same kind of difficulties over and over, even if we have already consciously unearthed their origins in early childhood.

As adults, when an event happens that contains familiar stimuli, it is associated with events that originally created the pathways. At this point, as Alkon says, "a massive chorus of electrical responses rises up,"[3] which determines thought, emotion, physical response, and even action. Therefore, our attitudes, beliefs, and fears are not easily erased by enlightened teachers, friends, therapists, clergy, or "good ideas."

An example of how this works is in the primal area of fear. Fear is a good place to start in our understanding of the persistence of (and possible freedom from) our core beliefs and habits because fear is so basic. In fact, I believe that all of our dysfunction and sin, all of our destructiveness, unhappiness, distraction, and lack of spiritual centeredness, arises out of fear. It is fear that gives rise to anger, control, anxiety, defensiveness, isolation, and everything else that keeps us apart from our true self, from others, and from God.

Fear is at the root of all that plagues us in the silence of contemplation as well. In meditation we come to observe the precise ways in which our mind and heart are afraid, and we confront what we are conditioned to do as a way of managing that fear. Over and over we observe our endless attempts to plan, understand, worry, control, and escape. Fear actually generates all of this pointless mental and emotional activity, and we may seem powerless to stop it.

Again, if our conditioned core belief is that life is dangerous and that we are a victim, we might discover in contemplation that we have continual thoughts about potential threats. Scenarios spin through our minds, weaving a drama of danger and of how we might move through these imagined circumstances in a way such that we will not get hurt. Or we might worry compulsively about perceived slights and nurse the many wounds that we have recently endured. This is fear in action. Alternatively, if our conditioned belief is that we are abandoned and alone in life and that it is up to us to create our own way, we might discover in our prayer that we engage in endless planning sessions. Fear drives this pointless activity, and we have no control over it.

Because human imperfection and sin are universal, so are pain and fear. None of us is exempt from some degree of damage. No matter how ideal our family of origin may have been, no matter how happy our childhood, there is always the residue, however small, of brokenness and fear. This is one way of understanding the doctrine of original sin. Born into a world that is not only beautiful and good, but also pervasively broken, we are hurt, and so we fear. Out of our fear, then, we live with some level of sin and dysfunction, hurting others in turn. The cycle of original sin continues, and it will continue forever. Such is the nature of our humanity.

We may experience our fear simply in the form of a little anxiety that is always under the surface, or in certain situations that cause us not to be at our best. Particular people may trigger a bit of anger for us, or we may live with a vague sense of emptiness from time to time. Because we are afraid, we develop strategies, even mild and seemingly benign ones, to help us cope. We eat a little too much when we are anxious; we lash out unintentionally; we retreat into our shell; we avoid conflict; we work too hard; we feel bad about ourselves and resolve to be a better person. These strategies get us into trouble, and they block happiness, trust, love, and openness to life.

Fear is also pervasive because it has been central to our evolution as a species. Without a fear that arises from pain, an animal would never learn to avoid certain dangerous environments. It is a useful tool, intended to help us survive. When we are hurt, fear motivates us to seek solutions, or to adjust, hide, manipulate, strike back, or whatever else we found in early childhood to be successful. We all learned, however dramatically or subtly, how to survive and get what we needed emotionally, even physically, in our family of origin.

These habits of belief, thought, emotion, relationship, and behavior—and fear—become permanently embedded in billions of neural connections very early on. In fact, there are powerfully swift, very direct neural pathways that bypass the *cortex* (the seat of rational thought) and go directly from perceived stimuli to the *amygdala* (the command center of fear). The amygdala then sends out chemical signals to the cortex and the body to think and to do what is necessary to survive. If an animal goes to a stream and is attacked by another animal, it learns to associate danger with the stimuli of running water, particular bushes, the angle of the sun, and specific smells and sounds. When these stimuli occur again in combination, they stimulate, through the amygdala, the fear response. Evolution is ingenious and powerful. The animal survives because its brain has short-wired normal processing through an express route from stimuli to amygdala to action.

These fear-based neural pathways, because they are linked by our evolution to survival, are much stronger and faster than others. The pathway that moves from the amygdala to the cortex is much shorter and more efficient than the pathway that moves from the cortex to the amygdala. Another way of putting this is that we move from fear to thought and action much more quickly and automatically than we move from rational thought into our fear. Emotions, especially fear, tend to dominate reason.

As a result, these very sophisticated, fear-based neurological habits, which developed through evolution, serve a useful purpose: survival. Perhaps they were particularly useful for us as children, since they helped us to survive the environment in which we found ourselves. As we grow, however, we continue to use them indiscriminately, even when they are not useful, because they are hard-wired into our brain. A cycle that began with pain, moved into fear, and then generated survival strategies may have helped us when we were young children in a bewildering environment, but when these habits are used in situations where they are really not needed, they distort our view of reality, and we end up separated from the truth, from our genuine and free self, from others, and from God. Because of our distortions, we hurt ourselves and others. That is when learned survival patterns become destructive. As such, our conditioned fear is the basis of sin, emotional distress, and evil.

ACCEPTING OUR BROKENNESS

Fear-based neural pathways cannot be erased. They are too powerful, too central to our survival as a species. They will always, therefore, be a part of the hardwiring of our brain. What this says is that our primary, fear-based brokenness is permanent, a part of our brain's very structure. Persons who have regularly but inconsistently been beaten may always, at some level, have a tendency to be on their guard. Others who never got what they needed unless they became helpless and desperate may forever employ this device. One who is abandoned emotionally may always feel ultimately alone. A person who received conditional love may always, to some degree, try to please. Each one of us has our own history, our own conditioning in the school of pain and fear, and each of us will respond for the rest of our lives to familiar fearful stimuli in familiar ways.

While all of this may seem awfully deterministic, it is not entirely so. Herein lies our hope: while we may live forever with our particular legacy of pain and fear, we can learn to recognize it, to name it, and to move out of its gripping cycle of thought, emotion, and behavior. We may always live with the effects of original sin that are specific to our circumstances, but upon the wound scar tissue can form. It will always be a little tender, at least, but we can grow and change to the point that when this scar is touched, it no longer hurts us with the same raw intensity as before. We can find healing, but our pain and fear will always retain some residue and the potential to resurface. We cannot erase it.

Core to the basic Christian doctrine is the fact of human sinfulness. We are alienated, separated, even as we come to know our essential goodness and union with our Creator. Pseudo-Macarius, a Syrian desert monk who was well-acquainted with contemplative union and advanced states of divine bliss, put it quite clearly: "I have not seen any perfect Christian or one perfectly free. Although a person may be at rest in grace and arrive at experiencing mysteries, revelations and the immense consolation of grace, nevertheless, sin still abides in him." [4]

The countercultural *People's Guide to Mexico* humorously proclaimed on its cover, "Wherever you go, there you are!" [5] Nearly two millennia before, Amma Theodora similarly taught her disciples that one could never get away from sin. Especially she taught that one could not do this by attempting external change:

There was a monk, who, because of the great number of his temptations, said, "I will go away from here." As he was putting on his sandals, he saw another man who was also putting on his sandals and this other monk said to him, "Is it on my account that you are going away? Because I go before you wherever you are going." [6]

To be plagued our whole life long by temptation, failure, sin, and brokenness is not necessarily a bad thing. In fact, it can be our saving grace as human beings. In our failures we are brought to humility, and to discover our need for God. In the particular way that pain and fear has taken shape in us, we have a way of opening ourselves to human *and* divine love. It is through our wounds that we may be touched deeply. In our vulnerability, our lack of control, we can be open to our need for God and other people. It is this sense that causes Navajo weavers to customarily thread a stray piece of yarn, a defect, into the otherwise perfect rug, so that there is a place where the Spirit can enter. Our wounds can certainly drive us away from spiritual and emotional health, but they can also drive us *toward* God and healing. The portal of our brokenness offers a way to transformation, even though we are reluctant to look for it there. To be sure, spiritual healing also happens through a realization of our innate goodness, strength of character, positive forms of devotion, and joy. Nevertheless, at the center of the Christian life stands, not a confident, beatific, smiling face, but the cross and resurrection. Our tradition witnesses to the dark and wondrous mystery of transformation through suffering.

As our familiar difficulties present themselves over and over, as we struggle with our powerlessness to change, and as we finally understand and, in the moment, fully experience and admit our ineffectual coping strategies that are born of fear, something opens up and grace flows into us. While we may be gifted by grace with certain strengths and abilities, it can also be through our weakness that we are transformed. Precisely through our brokenness, God's power becomes manifest as we are able, finally, to admit our need for it.

Saint Paul spoke very personally about frustration with his own weakness and his eventual discovery that it was, in fact, a place of grace:

> To keep me being too elated, a thorn was given me in the flesh, a messenger of Satan to torment me, to keep me from being too elated. Three times I appealed to the Lord about this, that it would leave me, but he said to me, "My grace is sufficient for you, for power is made perfect in weakness." So, I will boast all the more gladly of my weaknesses, so that the power of Christ may dwell in me.... for whenever I am weak, then I am strong. (2 Cor. 12:7b–10)

Anthony the Great, one of the earliest of the desert fathers, even went so far as to say that our weaknesses are necessary to salvation: "Whoever has not experienced temptation cannot enter into the kingdom of heaven. Without temptation, no one can be saved." [7]

THERAPY, CONTEMPLATION, AND NEUROLOGICAL CHANGE

How, exactly, are our pain, fear, and weakness transformed into God's strength, into wholeness and holiness? How do we move from neurologically conditioned core beliefs and patterns of limiting thought, emotion, and behavior into the freedom of life in God?

One model of deep change that is visible in our culture is long-term psychodynamic therapy. I introduce this model at this point because it is much more familiar to many in our day than the model of contemplative transformation. If we can more easily understand how basic change (even neurological change) happens in the context of therapy, perhaps we can transfer this understanding to the inner life of prayer. I am convinced that on some levels the process of change is the same in both contexts.

In the therapeutic setting, fears and other forms of brokenness are opened up, experienced, and understood. This is all done in the context of the relationship with the therapist. In this relationship a safe place is created where unhealthy and unhappy patterns of one's current experience can come to light, and the roots of these patterns can be explored.

In this safe place patients reexperience their core pain in the new context of compassion, challenge, questioning, understanding, and acceptance. Old patterns "enter the room." That is, they start to be transferred to the relationship with the therapist. They become current, so that in this new moment they may be experienced anew. Since the therapist responds with acceptance, commitment, and compassion instead of the kind of behavior that created the client's original difficulty, the old patterns can now result in a different outcome. Instead of more pain, there can be a healing of the patterns themselves.

A powerful example of the same healing process is found in contemplative prayer. In prayer there is also a new relationship, a safe environment to reexperience old patterns. As we sit quietly in relationship to God, the Spirit questions, and challenges, but ultimately accepts and has compassion, so that we come to associate new outcomes with the old patterns. Our fear arises as we observe the content of our thinking and feeling. A lack of control and frustration with ourselves surfaces. Our intolerance and impatience reveals itself. Now, however, instead of being met with a hurtful, reinforcing presence, they are met with openness and understanding in the new relationship with the Spirit.

In both cases our neurology is undergoing a slow but deeply profound change. We are doing nothing less than weighting and arborizing our neural pathways as we make new associations with old pain. As information streams along these pathways, we form, very slowly, new directions in which thought patterns can travel. Eventually, the familiar stimuli that usually cause us difficulty in life may move us instead into peace and health.

In her book *The Talking Cure*, Susan Vaughan presents a useful summary of how psychodynamic therapy changes our neurology and, therefore, affects our experience of life. In examining her summary, it is possible to consider, alongside it, how God's grace through contemplation does the same things. Here is the process.

One: In therapy we gain insight about our patterns. By observing our behavior and the recounting of our background and current situation, by listening to ourselves make associations, we gain insight about ourselves. We see patterns of thought and emotion, we observe our recurring story (or core belief) about ourselves, and we notice how we respond to life.

Contemplative prayer does the same thing as we watch the content of our mind and emotional reactivity. In the silence we see, over and over again *ad nauseam*, the patterns of thinking that represent our false, damaged self desperately at work, trying to manage life. Gradually, these patterns lead us deeper into our false core beliefs, which are based in fear and are, as such, the root of all our problems. By doing this, we actually observe the deeply ingrained neural pathways in action. We see clearly just how automatically our brain jumps from familiar stimuli to predictable results. As Vaughan points out, insight is initially frustrating because we think that, if we can see what we are doing, we should be able to stop it and do something different. Change, however, is not so easy or swift.

Insight about ourselves can be humiliating. We may look in horror at ourselves, because we have never realized the depth and pervasive quality of our fear, passivity, anger, tendency to control, escapism, or other "negative" qualities. This painful self-awareness, however, is part of the work of the Spirit within; it is part of the divine relationship that leads to healing. It is what we call, in our tradition, God's judgment. If we think of judgment as critical thinking, as the capacity to judge what is true, then we might be able to embrace this judgment, this insight. In contemplative prayer we are brought into reality, into truth, by the presence of the Spirit, who is truth. We are given eyes to see as God sees, and this is all done in the context of divine love and acceptance. As Jesus said, "You will know the truth, and the truth will make you free" (John 8:32).

Two: Within the context of the therapeutic relationship, we experience, name, and then question the patterns. Clients talk about what they do, how they re-create their life story, over and over, including in the present moment, even within the relationship with the therapist. Therapists question their clients' versions of their life stories, probing not only their origins but also their reality. Is this really the way life is, or is it the way the client perceives life to be? Is the patient creating and then endlessly reinforcing her or his own painful reality? Was the core belief understandable in its childhood creation but ultimately false and damaging?

Contemplative prayer does this same thing by enabling us to experience our patterns and core beliefs in the moment of silence, to name (and thereby objectify) them, and to question them. After saying to God, "I must hold on to anger," for the hundredth time, we begin to look differently at what our brain seems to believe and constantly regenerate. We question the reality of our reality. This, too, is a part of the challenging judgment of God. The Spirit within stops us mid-pattern and says, "Is this real, or are you just carrying on in an habitual way? Who are you? Are you your thoughts, or are you something that transcends them?"

The great fourth-century monk (and psychologist, really) Evagrius knew the benefit of questioning our thoughts in prayer as a way of understanding that we are more than they: "Be the door-keeper of your heart and do not let any thought come in without questioning it. Question each thought individually: 'Are you on our side or on the side of our foes?' And if it is one of ours, it will fill you with tranquillity." [8]

In the prayer of the heart, tradition calls us to "guard the heart," our true self in Christ, by "watching the mind." When we watch the mind, we reveal, examine, and question what it is doing habitually. By doing this, we protect the "heart" from being a victim of the false self and what it wants us to believe.

In the seventh century, Isaac of Nineveh continued in this same desert monastic tradition of discernment of thoughts in prayer: "Do not chase after [dark thought] and do not accept it either, but pray about it earnestly. Do not cease to call upon the Lord and he will show you whence it comes." [9]

When we do this, we actually interrupt the usual flow of neural pathways; we back up and halt their fulfillment. By observing, naming, and objectifying our thoughts—rather than being carried along by them in our usual way—we stop the pattern midway in its flow. This opens up the possibility that information may be able to flow in a new direction, toward a new end. Anger may result in awareness rather than frantic judgmentalism. Avoidance may move into stillness instead of escapist fantasies. Instead of our consciousness being taken captive along the pathways where our habitual patterns want to go, we may simply stop. By sitting still, rather than going along with the momentum of our neural impulses, we break into the new pathways. The habits of our brain are slowly changed.

Contemplation, when expanded beyond the sitting time into our daily lives, brings profound change in our external behavior as well. With contemplative awareness, we gain the capacity to stop ourselves mid-stream in a pattern of behavior or conversation, notice our systems at work, question them, and then find ourselves naturally moving to a different outcome.

And so in either case, whether we are speaking of internal awareness of thought and emotional reactivity or external awareness of behavior and speech, we simply step off the train. With awareness, we refuse the opportunity of yet another ride to an all-too-familiar destination. This, too, is grace at work, as the Spirit within gives us the power to stop, see the truth, and be still. Being still, refusing the ride, is no small thing. It takes courage because, if we get off the train, we will not know, at least initially, where we are. We find ourselves stranded in a wilderness of emptiness. We find ourselves in unknown, uncharted territory. God asks us to trust this territory. By leaving behind our habitual patterns of thought and reactivity, we leave behind our illusion of control. We float in the full emptiness of God's control. This is difficult, and we have much resistance to it.

The reason for this resistance is that in this empty, open place the self is not a factor. Many think of contemplative prayer as a way to become something better, as if by practicing it they could change the "bad" self for a "good" self. Contemplation, instead, is really a way of dying to the self, "bad" or "good." And so in the silence, we are not reconstructing a more desirable self. We are opening to no-self, where God's grace can have room to become manifest. In dying to self, the divine life that has always been within us can arise and become known. So contemplative prayer is a way of stopping the continual work of the false self, of stopping and being open to the no-thing that is God's life.

When we do manage to stop our mental momentum with objective awareness, it is as if the electrical charges within our neurons fire around, trying to connect to the next step, but are unable to do so. This disconnected feeling in our brain is anxiety. We do not know if anything other than our habitual patterns will "work." We float in the unfamiliar emptiness. Because our tendency is to rely upon memory that is already established, we disbelieve the new. And so we avoid the anxiety of disequilibrium, clinging to the familiar, even when it causes pain.

This anxiety and disequilibrium is the place of transformation. It is most powerfully represented for Christians, again, by the cross. The cross is the place of self-emptying, where control ends and surrender begins. The cross is the experience of not knowing, when we move out of our familiar patterns of power into nowhere, floating in God, dependent upon grace. New life emerges, resurrection comes, but not out of our own insight and activity. It comes from the new environment of trust in God.

Three: Within the context of the therapeutic relationship, we form and internalize new patterns. In therapy the client experiences the same old stimuli that life always presents. Reinforced, conditioned views of reality are continually re-created and made manifest in the present by the circumstances of life. People can be difficult. Our plans and intentions get frustrated. Crises come. Now, though, we are in a new relationship with the therapist, someone who is accepting, challenging, and compassionate, and we experience these old stimuli differently. This means that our old neural pathways find and establish new patterns of activity, so that such activity is in the compassionate, accepting atmosphere of divine love.

As the therapeutic relationship develops, it becomes internalized in the client. Between sessions the client begins to think about the therapist: what the therapist would say, what questions might be asked, how she or he might be present in a given situation. The patient identifies with the therapist and begins to see himself or herself through the therapist's eyes. So it is with God. In the intense, regular time of prayer we learn to internalize the reality of God or Jesus. Between our prayer times we ask ourselves what Jesus might do in a given situation. We wonder how we might behave if we really understood that God was with us all the time. We begin to carry God around with us, just as the client carries the therapist. We begin to see with God's eyes.

Neurologically speaking, the new relationship, whether with the therapist or with God or Jesus, becomes encoded in the brain through new neural relationships. As we identify with the new relationship, we think differently. New neural patterns develop as the strength of existing synaptic connections become weighted differently, as they arborize and make new connections. Theologically speaking, God's presence actually begins to alter our brain. The internalized Spirit moves us out of old patterns into new ones as our consciousness identifies with the spaciousness of the Spirit instead of with our old habitual limiting self-image and core beliefs about our life.

Four: During the time we are undergoing therapy, we reflect more frequently and intensely on our daily life experience, providing more opportunities to reinforce what we are learning in therapy. In the joys and difficulties of daily life, we now see more and more examples of our patterns at work in the moment as they are happening. In this moment we question them, and the work of therapy is reinforced in many more moments than just during the time of appointment.

In contemplation, the real work happens when we take the self-awareness that we experience on the cushion out into the streets. We begin to change only when we start to treat all of our life as an opportunity really to experience our patterns of what we are thinking, feeling, and doing. Daily life then is filled with ample opportunity to reinforce new neural pathways.

Again, this is very hard work. Most of us would rather confine self-awareness to the therapist's couch or the meditation cushion. To open our eyes in awareness in our daily life means that all of life is prayer. All of life is held in the judgment and mercy of God. By doing this, we reinforce what takes place in the particular intensity of prayer.

Five: In therapy, we experience strong, painful feelings safely, without dying or disintegrating. This safety actually takes power away from the strength of emotional patterns. In the context of safety, we bring up, admit, and name things about our past or our self that we never thought we could reveal to anyone. The amazing thing is, the much-feared, deeply-buried monsters that we release into the room do not kill us! In the same way, when we were children we discovered that the terrifying sounds that we heard in the dark seemed to fade away in the safety of our mother's arms and the simple flip of a light switch.

In contemplative prayer we sit through some pretty difficult stuff. Things surface that we imagine will destroy us. Some things overwhelm us. Normally, in the course of everyday life we would find a way to distract ourselves from such intense difficulties in one way or another. In disciplined stillness, however, we do not give ourselves that option. We just sit, going through whatever pain we must. In the safety of God's presence, however, we discover much to our surprise that we do not blow up. Our hair does not catch on fire! On the contrary, we are eventually but inevitably led into peace by the loving grace of God.

What is happening neurologically as we sit through our difficulties, rather than relieving, escaping, or fulfilling them in predictable ways? We are strengthening new neural pathways, new routes that lead into peace and acceptance. By tolerating difficulty we break into the pattern that believes that, if we do not keep moving in the direction of our strategies, we will not survive. By not going along with our pattern, *by actually surviving*, we build new pathways of existence.

Liberated, Yet Always Human

This process of healing is truly transformative. Over time we find ourselves no longer captive to patterns that previously seemed intractable. In terms of prayer we discover that our contemplation moves from painful self-awareness into more and more spaciousness. Our prayer is dominated less and less by captivating patterns of emotion-thought that are born out of our conditioned core beliefs, and our prayer begins to be dominated more and more by openness to God. We move from self-awareness to worship.

Yet, even in this case, familiar thoughts, distractions, and fantasies will still manifest themselves, continuing to emerge from our core brokenness, which will always be a part of our humanity. This is because even if we have done in-depth therapy, even if we have done years of contemplative prayer, we will always be somewhat affected by our hard-wired neurological patterns. Even if our neural connections have been arborized and weighted differently, even if our old well-worn pathways have become weaker than they used to be, they will still keep firing away, taking our consciousness to familiar places. Given this fact, we will always see early mental and emotional patterns generating themselves at will in our contemplative silence. We will always be human. Contemplative freedom does not eliminate our particular patterns of human brokenness.

The persistence of these patterns can be discouraging if we think our task is to get rid of them. Instead, it is possible to recognize briefly this old friend who has come to visit us again, name the pattern, and return to the spaciousness of God around it. As Charlotte Joko Beck has said to me about her meditation: "I just let my mind do whatever it wants." [10] At this point in one's practice, after many hundreds of instances of recognition, naming, and experiencing old familiar patterns of neurological activity, the thoughts lose their power to dominate us, even though they reoccur. We are, at this point, able to experience the energy of neurological activity within the limitless space of God's life. While we may not *eliminate* our brokenness, we can experience *freedom* from it.

CONCLUDING THOUGHTS

I have described a process of healing, of freedom from self-limiting false views of the self. As has been stressed many times (it must be stressed because it is hard for us really to believe it), this particular process of freedom is not a matter of creating new, more positive core beliefs about ourselves in order to overcome and replace old ones. It is not about programming the mind and the heart to adhere to a more positive, desirable reality. It is about simply becoming free from all created (and therefore self-limiting) realities. Apophatic prayer (the *via negativa*) is really about dis-identifying with all forms of the self. Put in terms of psychology, it is about unlearning old patterns of the false self, but it is not about building up a newer, better self.

This is because apophatic spirituality recognizes that *all* created realities are ultimately limiting. No matter how desirable we think our new self might be, it is still a self-created reality and, as such, at least partly created out of our ego-driven broken-ness, attachment, and aversion. Apophatic spiritu-ality offers the challenge to move, by the grace of God, beyond self into selflessness, where we might experience the limitless reality of God, instead of the limited reality of the constructed self. Put simply in terms of Christian theology, we are saved by grace, not by good works.

In terms of the process described here, then, our contemplative healing takes place as the false and neurologically conditioned self is exposed, expe-rienced, and questioned. Through this process we learn to dis-identify with habitual ways of seeing ourselves and our life. We learn to see our men-tal and emotional habits as neurological energy born from our life experience rather than letting it define "who we are." We learn simply to accept this activity of habitual neurological energy for what it is, and we learn that we are not our thoughts and emotions.

In fact, we begin to see that what we *believed* to be solid and permanent (the conditioned "self") has no solidity, and no permanence. "It" is simply energy, moving through us. By exposing, experiencing, questioning, and thereby dis-identifying with this energy, we move it out of the illusion of solid permanence and return to its rightful place as energy moving through us.

This form of contemplation thus moves into what Joko Beck calls "the frozen mass of emotion-thought" and releases it, through experiential awareness, out of its boundaried *mass*, into pure energy. Shame, fear, anger, lust, and sadness become just a particular kind of energy in our bodies rather than *who we are*. Experienced as pure energy, these feelings can continue to move rather than being locked in a boundaried illusion of the self. As pure energy, they pass through us. Where do they go? They go into the empty space of being that surrounds all of our illusory, condensed images of self. They go into the freedom of God. We then return to this emptiness, the fulsome silence that is pure being. Different qualities of energy shoot through our consciousness like comets through space, and everything is held within the expansiveness of being. As Saint Paul said to the Athenians, "In [God] we live and move and have our being" (Acts 17:28).

As we sit in silence, we can learn to recognize our neurological patterns of compacted energy, which are our core beliefs, our limiting assumptions about ourselves and life. As these are exposed, experienced, and questioned, they simply leave us, at least for the moment. What is left behind is not a newly improved, better-constructed self, but no-self. What is left is the spaciousness of our life in God, which was always there from the beginning, surrounding and infusing our limited and condensed "self." As Christians, we say that by grace the false self is crucified as we journey into God. What is left is our true identity, which is Christ's life manifested through us. In fact, he was always there, all along, waiting for us to get out of the way.

Chapter 12

CENTERING PRAYER RETREATS

Thomas R. Ward, Jr.

CONTEMPLATIVE OUTREACH HAS been offering centering prayer retreats to an increasingly interested and diverse public. While many know that these retreats are available, I often find that those who have not participated are curious about what happens. In this chapter, I hope to offer some part of my own experience of these retreats, to describe their design and its intention, and to encourage those who are attracted to participate.

I made my first centering prayer retreat at St. Benedict's Monastery in Snowmass, Colorado, in 1991. Since that time, I have made at least one retreat in each subsequent year and in some years more than one. Prior to that first retreat, I had difficulty "finding time" to do a second prayer session each day. I discovered centering prayer while on sabbatical in 1988 through reading Basil Pennington's book *Centering Prayer.*[1] I taught myself the prayer, began practicing it once a day, offered classes on it in the parish that I was serving, and formed several support groups. In short I was ahead of myself: I was teaching what I did not really know (which is not unusual for me), and I was encouraging others to do what I was not fully doing myself. After that first retreat, however, I no longer had difficulty finding time for that second prayer session. It was as if the Spirit had blown away my resistances. An interior shift had taken place that was evident in my external action.

In the past sixteen years I have listened to many people describing their centering prayer pilgrimages. My own experience is not atypical. One becomes attracted to the prayer out of a longing for silence, or for a deeper relation with God, or through a mysterious attraction to solitude. One tries the prayer and experiences a "high" of sorts, but this high does not last. We find ourselves wanting to keep the discipline of twenty minutes twice a day, but more often than not failing in that intention. Paul's words come to mind: "I do not do what I want.... I can will what is right, but I cannot do it" (Rom. 7:15, 18). If we are so graced, a centering prayer support group is available to be with us as we struggle with this interior tension. If not, we may drop the practice altogether and later wonder why. Then, at some point, we attend a centering prayer retreat, and the obstacles to our following through on our intention fall away as something like scales fell away from Paul's eyes

(Acts 9:18). The practice assumes a regular place in our lives.

Thomas Keating has written about the origins of centering prayer and the place that these retreats have in the movement.[2] That story begins with the renewal of religious life that followed the Second Vatican Council and includes the interfaith dialogue that also began during that period. Keating invited a Zen master into the monastery where he was abbot (St. Joseph's Abbey in Spencer, Massachusetts) to speak and to give a retreat. For nine years after that initial visit, the Zen master returned to a nearby retreat house for subsequent conversation and retreats. For years Keating had noticed that the Christian contemplative tradition had not been as vital in our day as it had been in former eras. At the same time young people were coming to the monastery who had exposure to Eastern practices and were asking if the Christian tradition had anything comparable. The monks at Spencer designed a basic workshop to teach what they came to call "centering prayer." When Keating resigned as abbot at Spencer in the fall of 1981, he began to teach centering prayer himself. Then in the summer of 1983 he offered an experimental retreat at the Lama Foundation in New Mexico:

> For some time I had wanted to put together a Christian contemplative retreat that would be comparable to a Zen *sesshin*, with a significant amount of time spent in silent meditation, an

experiment that had not been done before in
the Christian tradition, as far as I was aware. [3]

The results surprised Keating and the participants,
many of whom are now leaders in Contemplative
Outreach. They felt that they were growing in their
relation to God, and they became bonded with one
another. Within months, Contemplative Outreach
emerged as a network to foster the contemplative
dimension of the Gospel.

While other components have evolved over time,
three designs form the basic progammatic core:
workshop, support group, and retreat. What is such a
retreat like? It is a pilgrimage of sorts. One leaves the
known and familiar for the unknown and the unfamiliar. When I made my first retreat in 1991, I was
serving a large downtown congregation in Nashville,
Tennessee. My wife and I had children who were
then twelve and eleven years old. Arranging to be
away from home and from work for ten days in and
of itself required a significant commitment of time,
money, and planning. I still remember the airplane
ride from Nashville to Denver and then from Denver
to Aspen, being met in the Aspen airport, and riding
from the airport to the monastery. There was the
light conversation with the staff person who met me
and the other retreatants, and the gentle exploration
of who these other people were and why they had
come on such a journey. After getting settled in our

lodgings, we gathered in what was called the ranch house to await the evening meal.

Leaving to go on such an initial retreat was difficult; entry into the dynamics of that new community was even more difficult. I felt uncertain and insecure. Not only did I want to know who these other people were and why had they come, I wanted to know if they would accept me with my limited experience of this prayer and of anything like this gathering. In the conversation before and during dinner that first evening I did not find my fellow retreatants very forthcoming. Most kept well within themselves and revealed only general information. I wondered if I should be there at all! It was not until the introductory session after dinner that I had a sense that I was in the right place with the right people.

There were twenty-two of us retreatants and three staff members. We sat in a circle and responded to Pat Johnson's invitation to say who we were and what brought us there. Then the brief stories tumbled out.[4]

"I am Lucy. I was raised as a good Roman Catholic. I went to Mass faithfully every week and had a child every year in the first five years of my marriage. When my husband left me three years ago for a younger woman, I found myself searching for God as I never had before. A friend introduced me to centering prayer. It has become the most important part of my day. I don't know what I would do without this practice. I am here because I feel called to go deeper."

"My name is Henry. I'm a retired accountant. I'm also a Presbyterian. My wife and I have two grown children. As I moved into the second half of life, I found an emptiness inside me that I tried to fill with drink and television and golf. But over time I discovered that nothing touched that emptiness until I began attending a centering prayer group at my church. That group took me in. At first I stayed because of the way the people were with me and with one another, but then the emptiness I had known before when I slowed down seemed filled with a contentedness I had not known before. I knew that it was this prayer. The language of the Bible came alive. I'm here because I have to be here."

"Joyce is my name. I was not raised in the church. When I was in college in the sixties, I took up transcendental meditation to relieve stress. I have been practicing ever since, but I know I am missing something. A friend told me about her experience of these retreats, and I knew I had to come." [5]

As I sat and listened to these brief narratives, I knew that I was in the right place with the right people. It was not that I had much in common with most of them in a social sense; I did not. It was that I had the same hunger in my heart that I could hear behind their words. Beyond that, I quickly came to trust Pat Johnson and the other retreat leaders. They knew what they were doing. At the end of that first evening, the community of the retreat had come into being, and we were ready to do the inner work of sitting.

As I have reflected on these retreats over the years, I have seen a pattern unfold that is not unlike other retreat experiences or even the dynamic of a good vacation. There is an entry period; then, a period when one is in the world of the retreat as if there were no other life; and then there is an exit period that begins a day or two before the retreat actually ends. The design of the retreat acknowledges and embodies these rhythms. For instance, in both the entry and exit periods there are fewer sessions of centering prayer than there are in the middle period. In the beginning we need to adjust to the rhythms of the retreat; in the end we need to ease our way back into the world from which we came. For a few days in the middle we are living in a rhythm of life that seems much closer to what our hearts desire than the fast-paced tempo of our lives in the world.

A generic retreat day focuses on three sets of three twenty-minute sessions of centering prayer interspersed with meditative walks. Other aspects of the day are designed to foster these experiences of resting in God. What follows is the schedule of a typical retreat day:

6:00	Rise
6:30	Three sessions of centering prayer
8:00	Breakfast
9:00	Eucharist
10:00	Teaching
11:00	Three sessions of centering prayer
12:30	Lunch
1:30	Rest, conferences, free time
2:00	Meditation in motion (optional)
3:00	Three sessions of centering prayer
4:30	Teaching
6:00	Dinner
7:00	Questions and answers
8:30	Compline
9:00	Silence

Some aspects of the design call for comment. The teachings take the form of videotapes, featuring Thomas Keating reflecting on one or another aspect of the spiritual journey. The design calls for there to be some cognitive elucidation of what the retreatants may be undergoing as they participate in this practice more deeply. While God does not act mechanically with individuals who are praying, generalizations can be made about one's experience of this prayer over time.

Ideally, a simple diet is in keeping with the intent of the retreat. Most meals are vegetarian. There is limited sugar. Every effort is made to meet the dietary needs of individual retreatants. The result is most often a cleansing of the body as well as the spirit.

The meditation-in-motion consists of stretching exercises that allow retreatants to evacuate some of the energy that such deep praying releases. One might choose to take some other form of exercise, such as jogging or walking, but it is important to allow the body to move after so much intense sitting.

The mid-afternoon conferences with a staff person allow an opportunity for a retreatant to name an issue in the presence of an experienced listener. These are brief periods, most often twenty minutes or so in length. They are not designed to be extensive spiritual direction. However, significant issues often emerge in the course of these retreats, and it is important to have a time and place for these to be aired.

The question-and-answer sessions do not occur every night. Their purpose is to allow the retreatants to explore what they are experiencing by giving voice to their questions and by listening to the questions of others. However, the real answers come from the prayer itself. As the desert mothers and fathers never tired of saying, "Go into your cell, and your cell will teach you everything."

On the nights when there are not such sessions, compline is said earlier, and retreatants return to their rooms in silence.

Silence is fundamental to these retreats. Except for structured occasions—such as the question-and-answer sessions, conferences with the staff, and reading at meals—silence is maintained through-out—at meals, in the halls, during exercise periods. On post-intensive retreats, even eye contact is eliminated. The idea here is to reduce external stimulation and support so that one might be more present to the One who is present and active within.

On the final night of the retreat, there is an exit ritual that serves an analogous purpose to the entry ritual of the first night. Retreatants have an opportunity to give voice to what they have experienced, to what they anticipate upon returning home, and to whatever else they choose so that they might close this retreat and make a transition to their lives in the world. Leaders encourage retreatants to ease back into their ordinary lives: move slowly, do not schedule too many events too soon, and describe the experience to the intimate others in their lives with great care. Extended retreats engender a deep opening within, and exiting retreatants need to be gentle with themselves and with others.

That we come to know the fruits of the Spirit, not so much in the time of prayer as in our life in the world, is a central teaching of the basic centering prayer workshop. If that is true of one's daily practice (and it is), it can be seen even more emphatically in relation to such an intensive retreat. As mentioned above, I was able to work a second session of centering prayer into my life with relatively little resistance following my first retreat, where that seemed impossible earlier. And other fruits are easily noticeable: an increased desire for silence, solitude, and simplicity of life, for instance, and an increased ability to act on this desire; a clearer awareness of what is more and less important in the ordinary demands of daily life; a less judgmental attitude toward others; and an increased desire and ability to serve those in need.

What can be said about the experience of the prayer itself during the retreat? It is best compared to an individual session of centering prayer. At first the thoughts that preoccupy me are my most immediate concerns in my ordinary life: issues in my family, my work, the world around me. As the retreat continues, the character of the thoughts becomes more archetypal and intense; they come from a deeper level. I begin to notice particular manifestations of a desire for power and control, affection and esteem, and security and survival. And I experience a deeper yearning for intimacy with God. Some time near the middle of the retreat I am usually overcome by tears, often not knowing why. As I work with my journal in some of the discretionary time that the retreat allows, I sense that God is inviting me to live into words from Matthew that I have known all my life:

> Come to me, all you that are weary and are carrying heavy burdens, and I will give you rest. Take my yoke upon you, and learn from me; for I am gentle and humble in heart,

and you will find rest for your souls. For my yoke is easy, and my burden is light. (Matt. 11:28–30)

I have known the language of justification by grace through faith since my seminary days, but still I have been inclined to judge my worth as a person on what I do, not on receiving God's love. With centering prayer it is as if God breaks down my defenses in the silence so that I might experience the reality that I have long known with my mind. Or—to use the categories that Thomas Keating holds before us—God deconstructs my false self so that my true self may begin to come to birth in the silence. Silence is God's first language.[6] Contemplation is resting in God.[7]

The Eastern Orthodox call such tears of compunction "the second baptism," and I associate this experience with the word "purgation" in the classical tradition of the Christian West. Through such purgation I return to my life in the world lighter, without so much emotional heaviness, and freer to respond to the opportunities for service with which my daily life presents me. It is as if the powerful language from Galatians were finding a place in my life: "I have been crucified with Christ; and it is no longer I who live, but it is Christ who lives in me. And the life I now live in the flesh I live by faith in the Son of God, who loved me and gave himself for me" (Gal. 2:19–20).

The paradigm for these retreats calls for ten days, but various places offer them in varying lengths. There are three-day retreats, which begin with a basic workshop and continue with additional prayer sessions, and there are now thirty-day retreats in some places that offer retreatants an even deeper experience of resting in God. While St. Benedict's Monastery in Snowmass, Colorado is the home of this movement and its retreats, retreats and classes are now offered throughout the United States and in several other countries.

The wind of the Spirit is blowing in our time, inviting us to the deeper life of the Trinity. Centering prayer is one faithful, proven way to respond. Centering prayer retreats offer those, who have had a taste of God in the silence and who are hungry for more, a way to deepen their life in Christ with others who share that hunger.

NOTES

Introduction

1. Mark A. McIntosh, *Mystical Theology: The Integrity of Spirituality and Theology* (Oxford: Blackwell, 1998), ix.
2. Paul Tillich, as quoted in Martin E. Marty, "The secular prophets of 1967 looked to today," *Context* 32:1 (January 1, 2000): 1–2.
3. McIntosh, *Mystical Theology*, 2.

Chapter 1: A Traditional Blend

1. Saint John of the Cross, *The Living Flame of Love* (London: T. Baker, 1919), stanza 3:26–56.
2. John Cassian, *Conferences* (XI), trans. Owen Chadwick, Classics of American Spirituality Series (New York: Paulist, 1985).
3. Francis de Sales, *Introduction to the Devout Life*, trans. John K. Ryan (New York: Harper, 1950), part 3.
4. See Saint John of the Cross, *The Living Flame of Love*, op. cit.
5. See Saint Thérèse of Lisieux, recently declared a doctor of the church, especially her autobiography, *Story of a Soul*, letters, and compiled sayings.
6. See Jean-Pierre de Caussade, *Abandonment to Divine Providence*, trans. E. J. Strickland (St. Louis: Herder, 1921).
7. See Evagrius, *Treatise on Prayer* (London: SPCK, 1954).

8. See Saint John of the Cross, *Living Flame of Love*, op. cit., stanza 1.

9. See Evagrius and the Hesychasts of the Eastern Orthodox tradition.

10. Saint Teresa of Ávila, *The Interior Castle*, trans. Benedictines of Stanbrook (London: T. Baker, 1921).

11. Saint Teresa of Ávila, *The Interior Castle*, op. cit., where she writes of the "Prayer of Quiet."

12. Saint Teresa of Ávila, *The Way of Perfection*, trans. Benedictines of Stanbrook (London: T. Baker, 1911), where she also writes of the "Prayer of Quiet."

13. See, for examples, the desert fathers and mothers, Saint Teresa of Ávila, and Dom John Chapman, OSB.

14. See William of Saint-Thierry and Matthias Scheeben, *The Mysteries of Christianity* (London: Herder, 1946).

15. Saint John of the Cross, *Living Flame*, op. cit., stanzas 8–14.

16. See Saint Bernard of Clairvaux and virtually all the Christian mystics.

17. See Saint Augustine's *City of God* and Saint Paul's theology of community (cf. 1 Cor. 12–13).

Chapter 2: Three Contemplative Waves

1. Bernard McGinn, *The Foundations of Mysticism* (New York: Crossroad, 1994).

2. Thomas Keating, *Open Mind, Open Heart: The Contemplative Dimension of the Gospel* (Warwick, N.Y.: Amity House, 1986).

3. Thomas Merton, *Contemplative Prayer* (Garden City, N.Y.: Image Books, 1971), 90.

4. Cited in Michael Mott, *The Seven Mountains of Thomas Merton* (Boston: Houghton Mifflin, 1984), 311.

5. Thomas Merton, *New Seeds of Contemplation* (New York: New Directions, 1961), 38–41.

6. Merton, *Contemplative Prayer*, op. cit., 25.

7. Thomas Keating, *Invitation to Love: The Way of Christian Contemplation* (Rockport, Mass.: Element Books, 1992), 130–131.

8. Keating, *Open Mind, Open Heart*, op. cit., 28–29.

9. Thomas Keating, *Intimacy with God* (New York: Crossroad, 1994), 57.

10. Ibid., 68–69.

11. Keating, *Open Mind, Open Heart*, op. cit., 99.

12. Ibid., 48–49.

13. Keating, *Intimacy with God*, op. cit., 71.

14. Keating, *Invitation to Love*, op. cit., 58.

15. Ken Wilber, *Up from Eden: A Transpersonal View of Human Evolution* (Boulder: Shambhala, 1981).

16. Keating, *Open Mind, Open Heart*, op. cit., 128.

17. Keating, *Invitation to Love*, op. cit., 12.

18. Ibid., 11.

19. Keating, *Intimacy with God*, op. cit., 116–117.

20. Keating, *Invitation to Love*, op. cit., 124–125.

21. Ibid., 124.

22. Keating, *Intimacy with God*, op. cit., 112, 118.

23. Thomas Keating, *The Kingdom of God is Like …* (New York: Crossroads, 1993), 100–101.

24. Thomas Keating, *Foundations for Centering Prayer and the Christian Contemplative Life* (New York: Continuum, 2002), 105.

25. Ibid., 106.

26. Merton, *New Seeds of Contemplation*, op. cit., 296–297.

27. Bernard McGinn, *The Flowering of Mysticism: Men and Women in the New Mysticism—1200–1350* (New York: Crossroad, 1998).

Chapter 3: There is Nothing
between God and You

1. *The Cloud of Unknowing*, trans. James A. Walsh, S.J., Classics of Western Spirituality (New York: Paulist, 1981).

2. Ben Okri, *The Famished Road* (New York: Anchor, 1993), 110.

3. Meister Eckhart, *The Essential Sermons, Commentaries, Treatises and Defense*, trans. Edmund Colledge and Bernard McGinn (introduction by Huston Smith), vol. 2, Classics of Western Spirituality (New York: Paulist; London: SPCK, 1981), 280.

4. *The Complete Works of Saint John of the Cross*, trans. E. Allison Peers, vol. 3: *The Living Flame of Love* (Glasgow: Anthony Clarke Books, 1953), 228.

5. Yushi Nomura, *Desert Wisdom: Sayings from the Desert Fathers* (Maryknoll, N.Y.: Orbis, 2001), 26.

6. Thomas Keating, in a videotaped interview at the 2002 Spiritual Formation Conference, *Discovering the Divine DNA* (New York: Trinity Television, 2003).

7. Richard Kieckhefer, "Meister Eckhart's Conception of Union with God," *Harvard Theological Review* 71:3–4 (July/October 1978): 203–225.

8. Athanasius, *The Life of Antony and the Letter to Marcellinus*, ed. and trans. R. C. Gregg, Classics of Western Spirituality (London: SPCK; Mahwah, N.J.: Paulist, 1980), 7–11.

9. Compare Jean Leclercq, François Vandebroucke, and Louis Bouyer, eds., *A History of Christian Spirituality*, vol. 2: *The Spirituality of the Middle Ages* (New York: Seabury, 1968), especially 3–30.

10. Donald X. Burt, *Let Me Know You: Reflections on Augustine's Search for God* (Collegeville, Minn.: The Liturgical Press, 2003), 86.

11. Thomas Keating, *Open Mind, Open Heart: The Contemplative Dimension of the Gospel* (New York: Continuum, 2004).

12. Contemplative Outreach, Ltd., International Resource Center, 973-838-3384; or visit their website at www.contemplativeoutreach.org.

Chapter 4: Beatrice Bruteau's "Prayer and Identity"

1. Beatrice Bruteau, *Radical Optimism: Rooting Ourselves in Reality* (New York: Crossroad, 1993; 2nd ed., Boulder, Colo.: Sentient, 2002); *God's Ecstasy: The Creation of a Self-Creating World* (New York: Crossroad, 1997); *The Easter Mysteries* (New York: Crossroad, 1995), as well as *What We Can Learn from the East* (New York: Crossroad, 1995).

2. This is the first of three essays in *The Contemplative Review* (all by Bruteau) in a special issue titled *Prayer: Insight and Manifestation*. The other two articles are "Insight and Manifestation: A Way of Prayer in a Christian Context" and "The Prayer of Faith."

3. From a paper given for a group of monks and visitors at the Abbey of Gethsemani, and later published as "Activating Human Energy for the Grand Option" in *Cistercian Studies* 19:2 (1984): 151–162, and as Chapter One in *The Grand Option: Personal Transformation and a New Creation* (Notre Dame, Ind.: University of Notre Dame Press, 1996).

4. Bruteau adds this note: This particular piece is the first in a trilogy. It deals with attaining the consciousness of the Formless, the Infinite, the Transcendent, the Absolute. The succeeding pieces deal with the Manifestation aspect of the Reality in the world of forms, finitude, and the relative. In my view these are

316 ※ SPIRITUALITY, CONTEMPLATION & TRANSFORMATION

the two aspects of the whole Real. These are comparatively old pieces of work, but I have continued to emphasize the presence of the two aspects *simultaneously*. A recent example is titled "Mysticism and Social Transformation," which is further developed to book-length in *The Holy Thursday Revolution* (Maryknoll, N.Y.: Orbis, 2005), following the natural-science book *God's Revolution: The Creation of a Self-Creating World*. I mention these lest readers form the impression that only the transcendent aspect is being recognized and appreciated. Current favorite images are Dancing Siva (quiescent Transcendent and Dancing manifested in the relative) and John 1:18—invisible emptiness (*kolpon*) and singly generated God exegeting.

5. This interpretation, which takes the Greek components *meta* and *noia* literally, has also been powerfully suggested by Marcus J. Borg in his book *The Heart of Christianity: Rediscovering a Life of Faith* (San Francisco: Harper, 2003).

6. I often refer to this as "the egoic operating system" because it comprises a basic hardwiring of perception. See my "Nurturing the Heart," *Parabola* 27:1 (Spring 2002): 6–11; and my CD series *Encountering the Wisdom Jesus* (Boulder, Colo.: Sounds True, 2005).

7. See, for instance, Sharon Begley, "How the Brain Rewires Itself," *Time* 169:5 (January 29, 2007): 79.

8. Cynthia Bourgeault, *Centering Prayer and Inner Awakening* (Cambridge, Mass.: Cowley, 2004).

9. The generic term "centering" was actually coined by Thomas Merton; what is now centering prayer was in its early days called "The Prayer of the Cloud," based on *The Cloud of Unknowing*.

Chapter 5: Reading Living Water

1. Psalm 2:1, *The Book of Common Prayer* (New York: Church Hymnal Corp., 1986), 586.

2. Wendell Berry. *Life is a Miracle: An Essay Against Modern Superstition* (Washington, D.C.: Counterpoint, 2000), 8.

3. Raimon Panikkar, *The Experience of God: Icons of the Mystery* (Minneapolis: Fortress, 2006), 20.

4. See Václav Havel, "The Spiritual Roots of Democracy," *Lapis: The Inner Meaning of Contemporary Life* (Summer 1995): 27–30, also published as "Democracy's Forgotten Dimension," *Journal of Democracy* 6:2 (April 1995): 3–10. See also Havel's "Politics, Morality, and Civility," in *Summer Meditations*, trans. Paul Wilson (New York: Vintage Books, 1992), 1–20.

5. This description of contemplative prayer is taken from a collective statement by twelve teachers of the practice at a gathering in Snowmass, Colorado, in October 2002, co-sponsored by Father Thomas Keating and David G. R. Keller, coordinator of the Contemplative Ministry Project.

6. A profound description of the process of transformation, including its psychological dimension, can be found in Thomas Keating's *The Better Part: Stages of Contemplative Living* (New York: Continuum, 2002), especially Chapter Five.

7. Although many citations could be listed, several biblical descriptions of transformed life are: Romans 12:1–21, 1 Corinthians 12 and 13, Galatians 5:16–26, Philippians 2:1–18, and Colossians 3:1–17. The writings and public teaching of Thomas Keating are centered on the fruits of the Spirit as consequences of human transformation.

8. Laurence Freeman, quoting John Main, in *Light Within: The Inner Path of Meditation* (New York: Crossroad, 1987). 31.

9. From a discussion between Thomas Keating and Larry Todd Wilson, October 2005. Used with permission.

10. This perspective had a major influence in the development of Anglican theology and piety, especially in the writings and preaching of Lancelot Andrewes and Richard Hooker. Sadly, this central Gospel message has not been emphasized in modern Anglican theological education. For a detailed description of this influence, see A. M. Allchin, *Participation in God: A Forgotten Strand in Anglican Tradition* (Greenwich, Conn.: Morehouse-Barlow, 1988).

11. "That Nature is a Heraclitean Fire and of the Comfort of the Resurrection," in Gerard Manley Hopkins, *Selected Poems*, ed. Peter Feeney (Oxford: Oxford University Press, 1994), 47.

12. For a collection of sayings by and narratives about the desert fathers and mothers see Benedicta Ward, *The Sayings of the Desert Fathers: The Alphabetical Collection* (Kalamazoo, Mich.: Cistercian, 1975). For an introduction to the life and wisdom of the desert elders, see David G. R. Keller, *Oasis of Wisdom: The Worlds of the Desert Fathers and Mothers.* (Collegeville, Minn.: The Liturgical Press, 2005).

13. Dorotheos of Gaza, "On Renunciation," I, in *Discourses and Sayings*, trans. Eric P. Wheeler (Kalamazoo, Mich.: Cistercian, 1977), 77 and 79.

14. Tim Vivian, "Witness to Holiness: Abba Daniel of Scetis," *Coptic Church Review* 24:1–2 (2003): 22.

15. Panikkar, *The Experience of God*, op. cit., 132–134.

16. Vivian, "Witness to Holiness," op. cit., 22.

17. Ibid., 23.

18. The meaning of the Greek word ασκεω is to "care for." Ascetic life is a discipline of caring for the full-

ness of God in us. An ascetic is a person who cares for their true self.

Chapter 6: Binding Head and Heart

1. *The Book of Common Prayer* (New York: Church Hymnal Corp., 1979), 388.
2. See Henri J. M. Nouwen, *Out of Solitude* (Notre Dame: Ave Maria, 1987).
3. From a lecture by the patristic scholar Father Godfrey Diekmann, OSB, at St. John's School of Theology/Seminary, Collegeville, Minnesota.
4. A. M. Allchin, *The World is a Wedding: Explorations in Christian Spirituality* (New York: Oxford University Press, 1978), 78.
5. See Evelyn Underhill, "The Parish Priest and The Life of Prayer," in *Life As Prayer and Other Writings of Evelyn Underhill*, ed. Lucy Menzies (Harrisburg: Morehouse, 1991), 121–122. Adapted for inclusive language by the author.
6. John Main, *The Heart of Creation* (New York: Crossroad, 1989), 29.
7. For an excellent study demonstrating the integration of Christian thought and prayer in the early church, see Robert Louis Wilken, *The Spirit of Early Christian Thought: Seeking the Face of God* (New Haven: Yale University Press, 2003).
8. See Evelyn Underhill, *Life As Prayer*, op. cit., Chapter Seven, "The Priest's Life of Prayer" and "Life of Prayer in the Parish," 121–156.
9. Mother Mary Clare, SLG, *Encountering the Depths* (Harrisburg, Penn.: Morehouse, 1993), 5.
10. See Henri Le Saux/Abhishiktananda, cited in *The Fire of Silence and Stillness,* ed. Paul Harris (Springfield, Ill.: Templegate, 1995), 179–180.

11. The Snowmass participants were Jeannette Bakke, Cynthia Bourgeault, Tilden Edwards, Laurence Freeman, Thomas G. Hand, Glenn Hinson, Thomas Keating, David Keller, Patrick Mitchell, Richard Rohr, Helen Rolfson, Nancy Roth, and Mary White. Unfortunately, Father Keating was ill with pneumonia and could not participate and Father Laurence Freeman, OSB, was not able to attend because of an abbatial election in his monastic community. Both men are active participants in the ongoing life of the Contemplative Ministry Project. Diane Fassel was process facilitator at Snowmass.

12. The quotations that follow are from "Binding Head and Heart," drafted by participants on October 2–6, 2003. Summaries of the dialogue can be found at the Contemplative Ministry Project in Healdsburg, California, St. Benedict's Monastery in Snowmass, Colorado, and The Trust for the Meditation Process in Minneapolis, Minnesota.

13. Persons interested in participating in the project's goals and conversations and receiving more detailed information about the results of the Snowmass gathering and subsequent activities may write to The Contemplative Ministry Project, 810 Gromo Court, Healdsburg, CA 95448, or e-mail contempminproj@earthlink.net.

Chapter 7: Centering Prayer and the Work of Clergy and Congregations

1. Edwin Friedman, *A Failure of Nerve: Leadership in the Use of the Quick Fix*, ed. Edward W. Beal and Margaret M. Treadwell (Bethesda, Md.: The Friedman Estate and Trust, 1999), 112–120.

2. Barbara Ehrenreich, *Fear of Falling: The Inner Life of the Middle Class* (New York: Pantheon, 1989).

3. Edmund Gibbs, *Church Next: Quantum Changes in How We Do Ministry* (Leicester: InterVarsity, 2001), 18–19.
4. *The Book of Common Prayer* (New York: Church Hymnal Corp., 1979), 557–565.
5. Thomas Keating, *Invitation to Love: The Way of Christian Contemplation* (Rockport, Mass.: Element, 1992), 6–8.
6. Thomas Keating, *Intimacy with God* (New York: Crossroad, 1994), 77.
7. Julian of Norwich, *The Showings* (New York: Paulist, 1978), 225.

Chapter 8: Seeking a Deeper Knowledge of God

1. *The Book of Common Prayer* (New York: Church Hymnal Corp., 1979), 857.
2. *The Book of Common Prayer*, op. cit., 13.
3. William Porcher DuBose, *Turning Points in My Life* (New York: Longmans, Green and Company, 1912), 20.

Chapter 9: Spirituality, Contemplation, and Transformation

1. Thomas Keating, *Open Mind, Open Heart: The Contemplative Dimension of the Gospel* (New York: Continuum, 1986, 2006), 19.
2. Thomas Keating, *Fruits and Gifts of the Spirit* (New York: Lantern Books, 2000), 3–4.
3. Robert Frost, *Complete Poems of Robert Frost* (New York: Holt, Rinehart and Winston, 1964), 386.

4. Wade Clark Roof, *A Generation of Seekers: The Spiritual Journeys of the Baby-Boom Generation* (San Francisco: Harper Collins, 1993), 78–79.

5. Mark A. McIntosh, *Mystical Theology: The Integrity of Spirituality and Theology* (Oxford: Blackwell, 1998), ix.

6. Thomas Merton, *The Climate of Monastic Prayer* (Spencer, Mass.: Cistercian Publications, 1969), 152.

7. Keating, *Open Mind, Open Heart*, op. cit., 19.

8. Ibid.

9. As quoted in Merton, *The Climate of Monastic Prayer*, op. cit., 65–66.

10. M. Basil Pennington, *Centering Prayer: Renewing an Ancient Christian Prayer Form* (Garden City, N.Y.: Image Books, 1982), 30–32.

11. Thomas Keating, *Intimacy with God* (New York: Crossroad, 1994), 47.

12. Keating, *Open Mind, Open Heart*, op. cit., 4.

13. Keating makes a clear distinction between *lectio divina* and centering prayer.

14. I draw attention to the difference between "contemplation" and "centering prayer" further down. The distinction is Thomas Keating's, and it is important to his work and those praying in this way.

15. Keating, *Intimacy with God*, op. cit., 124.

16. Keating, *Open Mind, Open Heart*, op. cit., 4.

17. Keating, *Intimacy with God*, op. cit., 11.

18 *The Collected Works of St. John of the Cross*, trans. Kieran Kavanaugh and Otilio Rodriguez (Washington, D.C.: Institute of Carmelite Studies, 1979, 2nd ed.), 318.

19. William Johnston, ed., *The Cloud of Unknowing* (New York: Image, 1973), 54–56.

20. *The Book of Common Prayer* (New York: Church Hymnal Corp., 1979), 236.

21. Ibid., 846.

22. Keating, *Open Mind, Open Heart*, op. cit., 128.

23. Keating, *Intimacy with God*, op. cit., 98.

24. Keating, *Open Mind, Open Heart*, op. cit., 127.

25. Ibid.

26. Ibid., 128.

27. Thomas Keating, *Manifesting God* (New York: Lantern Books, 2005), 88.

28. Keating, *Intimacy with God*, op. cit., 153.

29. Keating, *Open Mind, Open Heart*, op. cit., 130.

30. Ibid., 15.

Chapter 10: Keep the Rest

1. George Herbert, *The Complete English Works* (New York: Knopf/Everyman, 1995), 156.

2. Anne Lamott, *Traveling Mercies: Some Thoughts on Faith* (New York: Anchor Books, 1999), 142.

3. John Tarrant, *The Light Inside the Dark: Zen, Soul, and the Spiritual Life* (New York: HarperCollins, 1998), 27–28.

4. Thomas Merton, *Contemplative Prayer* (New York: Doubleday, 1996), 89.

5. Mark Jarman, "Unholy Sonnets" (#4), from *Questions for Ecclesiastes* (Ashland, Ore.: Story Line Press, 1997), 54.

6. Thomas Keating, *The Better Part: Stages of Contemplative Living* (New York: Continuum, 2000), 60.

7. Thomas Keating, *Invitation to Love: The Way of Christian Contemplation* (New York: Continuum, 1992), 56.

8. Herbert, *The Complete English Works*, op. cit., 184.

9.   Belden Lane, "Stalking the Snow Leopard: A Reflection on Work," in *The Solace of Fierce Landscapes* (New York: Oxford, 1998), 80.

10. Keating, *The Better Part*, op. cit., 50.

11. Merton, *Contemplative Prayer*, op. cit., 59.

Chapter 11: Changing Your Mind

1.   As a parish priest and author on subjects related to spirituality, my knowledge of neurology and psychotherapy is extremely limited. The intent of this essay is to illustrate some of the dynamic of what happens over time when one practices contemplative prayer, using a neurological model simply in order to suggest something of the incarnated, physical reality that is involved in spiritual transformation.

2.   Daniel L. Alkon, *Memory's Voice: Deciphering the Brain-Mind Code* (New York: HarperCollins, 1992).

3.   Ibid.

4.   Homily 8, Pseudo-Macarius, *Fifty Spiritual Homilies, and The Great Letter*, trans. George A. Maloney (New York: Paulist, 1992), 83.

5.   Carl Franz, *People's Guide to Mexico* (Santa Fe, N.M.: John Muir, 1974).

6.   *The Sayings of the Desert Fathers*, trans. Benedicta Ward (Kalamazoo: Cistercian, 1984), 84.

7.   Ibid., 2.

8.   Evagrius of Pontus, *Letter to Melania*, trans. Martin Parmentier (Utrecht: s.m., 1985), 115.

9.   Quoted by Olivier Clément, *The Roots of Christian Mysticism: Texts of the Patristic Era with Commentary* (New York: New City, 1995), 170.

10. Charlotte Joko Beck is the founder and spiritual leader of the Zen Center of San Diego in California.

Chapter 12: Centering Prayer Retreats

1. Basil Pennington, *Centering Prayer* (New York: Image Books, 1980).

2. Thomas Keating, *Intimacy with God* (New York: Crossroad, 1994), 11–21.

3. Keating, *Intimacy with God*, op. cit., 18. While it should be obvious that Christian orthodoxy gives shape to centering prayer in general and these retreats in particular, I have learned that some find Keating's participation in interreligious dialogue suspect and his admitted borrowings from the practices of other traditions unfaithful to his Christian roots. For a clear exposition of the theological underpinnings of this practice, see "The Theological Basis of Centering Prayer," *Intimacy with God*, 32–38.

4. Pat Johnson was one of the participants on the first retreat at the Lama Foundation. She soon moved to the vicinity of St. Benedict's to work with Keating. For almost twenty years Pat has led the retreats there and has had a vital role in designing and implementing retreats, as well advising others in this work. For instance, Johnson joined our group at St. Mary's Conference Center near Sewanee in June of 1997 when we offered our first retreat. We knew that much of the character of the retreats was in the details, and we wanted Johnson's steadying presence and counsel as we moved from what we intended to its implementation. I attribute much of the steady fidelity of the subsequent fifteen retreats to Pat's guidance.

5. While exceptions are made, a daily practice of centering prayer is a normative prerequisite for making such a retreat. Moving from little centering

prayer to four and half hours a day or more is not advisable.

6.   Thomas Keating, *Open Mind, Open Heart: The Contemplative Dimension of the Gospel* (New York: Continuum, 1997), 127–128.

7.   Ibid., 20.

About the Contributors

Cynthia Bourgeault is an Episcopal priest and a well-known retreat and conference leader. She is founding director of the Aspen Wisdom School, principal guest teacher for the Contemplative Society in Victoria, British Columbia, and a core faculty member of the Spiritual Paths Graduate Institute in Aspen, Colorado, and Santa Barbara, California. She is author of five books, including *Centering Prayer and Inner Awakening*.

Beatrice Bruteau is a philosopher active in the integrated study of science, mathematics, philosophy, and spirituality. She was on the editorial staff of *International Philosophical Quarterly* at Fordham University, where she also founded the Teilhard Research Institute and was active in the Cardinal Bea Institute of Spirituality.

David Frenette is a contemplative practitioner, counseling psychologist, and spiritual director, as well as an adjunct faculty member in the Religious Studies department at Naropa University. A student of Thomas Keating's since 1984, he co-founded, taught, and lived for ten years at a centering prayer retreat community under Father Keating's auspices.

He teaches centering prayer as a practical contemplative path for those in ordinary life, laying a foundation for a living non-monastic tradition of Christian contemplation. His approach is explored more fully at www.incarnationalcontemplation.com.

THOMAS KEATING, OCSO, entered the Cistercian Order in 1944. He was appointed Superior of St. Benedict's Monastery in Snowmass, Colorado, in 1958, and was elected Abbot of St. Joseph's Abbey in Spencer, Massachusetts, in 1961. He returned to Snowmass after retiring in 1981, where he established a program of intensive retreats in the practice of centering prayer.

DAVID G. R. KELLER is an Episcopal priest, the former Steward of the Episcopal House of Prayer at St. John's Abbey in Collegeville, Minnesota. He is currently Co-Chair of the Contemplative Ministry Project and an Adjunct Professor at the Center for Christian Spirituality at General Theological Seminary in New York City. He is the author of *Oasis of Wisdom: The Worlds of the Desert Fathers and Mothers.*

FR. JUSTIN LANGILLE is a contemplative Catholic priest, ordained in 1980 for the Diocese of San Diego. He has taught as a professor of Theology at the University of San Diego for over ten years. He is currently the Pastor of a small rural parish and serves as Spiritual Director for Contemplative Outreach of

San Diego, having been its regional coordinator for over fifteen years. He has served on the Board of Trustees for Contemplative Outreach International and is currently co-chair of the Retreat Faculty for this worldwide spiritual network.

PAUL DAVID LAWSON is Rector of St. Cross Episcopal Church in Hermosa Beach, California. He is also Area Coordinator for Contemplative Outreach Limited and on the Ecclesiastical Court for the Diocese of Los Angeles. He is the author of *Old Wine in New Skins: Centering Prayer and Systems Theory*.

TOM MACFIE is University Chaplain for The University of the South in Sewanee, Tennessee.

JENNIFER MICHAEL is Associate Professor of English in the College of Arts and Sciences at The University of the South in Sewanee.

BRIAN C. TAYLOR is the Rector of St. Michael and All Angels Episcopal Church in Albuquerque, New Mexico.

THOMAS R. WARD, JR. is a priest of the Episcopal Church. He is currently working with Contemplative Outreach, Ltd. in furthering the contemplative dimension of the Gospel.

OTHER TITLES OF INTEREST
FROM LANTERN BOOKS

FRUITS AND GIFTS OF THE SPIRIT

Thomas Keating, OCSO

THOMAS KEATING HAS spent over fifty years in sustained practice and devotion to the spiritual life. The results of this creative, humble activity are now summarized in this remarkable book, *Fruits and Gifts of the Spirit*.

As Father Keating says, the spiritual journey is a gradual process of enlarging our emotional, mental, and physical relationship with the divine reality that is present in us, but one not ordinarily accessible to our emotions or concepts. The spiritual journey teaches us: first, to believe in the Divine Indwelling within us, fully present and energizing every level of our being; secondly, to recognize that this energy is benign, healing, and transforming; and, thirdly, to enjoy its gradual unfolding step-by-step both in prayer and action.

ISBN: 9781930051218
PAPERBACK
$14.00
128 PAGES

Manifesting God

Thomas Keating, OCSO

T HIS BOOK PRESENTS the principles of contemplative prayer—the retreat into the "inner room" mentioned by Jesus in Matthew 6:6, where the individual is able to meet God. In the inner room, the silent space in which God unloads the burdens and false selves that govern our individuality and our daily lives, God acts as a divine therapist, healing us and forcing us to recognize how many barriers we put up between ourselves and an authentic relationship with God.

Abbot Keating explores what it means to enter the inner room and the transformation that takes place there. He explains the guidelines of centering prayer and offers advice on how to develop the relationship more deeply.

ISBN: 9781590560853
PAPERBACK
$14.00
144 PAGES

THE DIVINE INDWELLING
Centering Prayer and Its Development

Thomas Keating, OCSO

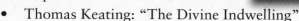

THESE ESSAYS DISCUSS several features of centering prayer and the contemplative outreach movement:

- Thomas Keating: "The Divine Indwelling"
- Thomas R. Ward: "Spirituality and Community: Centering Prayer and the Ecclesial Dimension"
- Sarah A. Butler: "Lectio Divina as a Tool for Discernment"
- George F. Cairns: "A Dialogue Between Centering Prayer and Transpersonal Psychology"
- Gail Fitzpatrick-Hopler: "The Spiritual Network of Contemplative Outreach Limited"
- Paul David Lawson: "Leadership and Changes Through Contemplation: A Parish Perspective"
- Thomas Keating: "The Practice of Intention/ Attention"

ISBN: 9781930051799
PAPERBACK
$10.00
112 PAGES

Centering Prayer and the Healing of the Unconscious

Fr. Murchadh Ó Madagáin

Fr. Murchadh Ó Madagáin describes the life and thoughts of Fr. Thomas Keating on Centering prayer. Fr. Murchadh Ó Madagáin traces its roots back to the fourth- and fifth-century Desert Fathers such as Evagrius and John Cassian. He shows how it was used in the medieval classic *The Cloud of Unknowing* and practiced by saints John of the Cross and Teresa of Avila, then revived by Thomas Merton during the twentieth century.

The book illustrates how, by bringing the insights of contemporary psychology to bear on this ancient method of prayer, Fr. Keating not only revitalized the contemplative tradition, but also enabled it to become a powerful tool for people of faith to gain insight into themselves and God, whom Keating calls the "divine healer."

ISBN: 9781590561072
PAPERBACK
$18.00
336 PAGES

AUTHENTICITY
Clearing the Junk: A Buddhist Perspective

Venerable Yifa

VEN. YIFA EXPLORES junk in all its ramifications—junk food, junk stuff, junk relationships, junk communication, and junk thoughts and feelings. She shows how our obsession with materialism, convenience, and the fast-paced nature of our society diminishes our ability to connect wholeheartedly with others, making it harder for us to lead authentic lives. By consciously separating out what is junk from what is genuine, she says, and through practicing right-mindedness, we can gain equanimity, clarity of purpose, true friendship, and the ultimate realization of our Buddha nature.

VENERABLE YIFA is a nun belonging to the religious order Fo Guang Shan, founded by Venerable Master Hsing Yun in Taiwan. Yifa lives at Hsi Lai temple in Hacienda Heights, California. She is a contributor to *Benedict's Dharma: Buddhists Reflect on the Rule of St. Benedict.*

ISBN: 9781590561096
PAPERBACK
$10.00
128 PAGES

THE TENDER HEART
A Buddhist Response to Suffering

Venerable Yifa

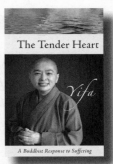

EXPLORING THE CENTRAL Buddhist concepts that life is full of suffering, everything is impermanent, and that everything in existence is connected, Venerable Yifa looks at how and why suffering occurs and how we can learn from tragedies to access even deeper spiritual truths. She reveals the Buddhist perspective on the nature of suffering, the meaning of justice, what is evil and what is good, and why some people die and others live.

Yifa elucidates Buddhism's eight different types of suffering from a practical standpoint, illuminating the essential Buddhist ideas of compassion and mindfulness, and shows how we can apply these principles to everyday life and in our relationships. Her aim throughout is to help us to reach out, to heal others, and to protect ourselves—to safeguard our hearts—when suffering strikes.

ISBN: 9781590561119
PAPERBACK
$10.00
128 PAGES

THE COMMON HEART
An Experience of Interreligious Dialogue

Edited by Netanel Miles-Yepez
Foreword by Ken Wilber
Introduction by
  Thomas Keating, OCSO

FOR TWENTY YEARS, a group of spiritual seekers from many religious traditions met in various places around the United States under the rubric of the Snowmass Conferences to engage in the deepest form of interreligious dialogue. The experience was intimate and trusting, transformative and inspiring. To encourage openness and honesty, no audio or visual recording was made of, and no articles were written about, the encounters.

When these encounters came to an end, it was agreed that reflections on what had happened emotionally, spiritually, philosophically, and theologically during the Snowmass dialogues should be written down. The result is *The Common Heart*.

ISBN: 9781590560990
PAPERBACK
$15.00
144 PAGES